Little Rays Of Light

Margaret Hunt

Messages of Healing, Comfort and Hope

I dedicate this book to my wonderful husband Graham, my soulmate, who puts up with all my funny little ways and eccentricities

Prologue

In the following pages you will find little messages of healing and I like to call them little messages of light for light flows from the words we share with each other whether they are spoken or written and that light radiates out to illuminate those areas which need healing.

This book is a compilation of some of my weekly blogs from recent years about healing on Facebook. I have been writing these blogs for a very long time and my purpose has always been to share healing practices, to share my own healing stories from my life, to share the healing from nature and at the same time to bring comfort and reassurance to others.

I love to tell stories and so I tell stories from the experiences of my life and also from my connections and communications with nature and my purpose is always to help people to empower and heal themselves.

We learn from life and we learn from one another and when we share our stories we can encourage others to find their own inner healing.

You can read this book as it is and enjoy the stories and the suggestions and the help to enable you to heal yourself or you can use it like a set of oracle cards where you just open the book and see which page you are being shown. Like an oracle card it will always be the perfect message for you for that time.

I have seen many little miracles in my life and many synchronicities and I never cease to be amazed by the magic which is always there waiting to reassure us and confirm for us that we are on the right track.

So pull up a comfortable chair and sit by the fire in a cosy cottage parlour with a kettle singing over the fire as it boils. Put hot water into a beautiful teapot and let it brew and when it is ready pour it into a rose patterned china teacup. Reach out for the delicious cake which is on a little table by the side of your armchair then sip your tea and eat your cake getting cosy in front of the fire and you will be ready to begin. I share my little miracles with you and may these words bring you much comfort, hope and healing.

The Fire

Of all the elements it is the fire which we are often very lacking in and sometimes we forget to constantly tend to our inner fire.

Many of our teachers bring their light in the form of fire or even flames; St Francis brings the Sapphire flame, Magdalene brings the lavender flame and she also brings her rainbow coloured fire; it is wonderful to work with all of these to bring us healing. However it is our own fire which is more important than anything else at all.

When your fire is burning brightly you never ever hold back from saying what you feel, you always speak the truth, you never push away your feelings and when you do own it you stand completely in your own power. When you stand in your own fire you feel it, there is no way you can not feel it.

When your fire flows you do not push anything down because when we repress our feelings or hold in our words the kundalini energies become squashed deep down within us and we lose the ability to spontaneously speak our truth.

Have you ever felt rage or anger rising up within you? This is the fire and it is not a negative energy and you are not meant to suppress it for it is there to be used to release what is underneath it. There may be times where you feel something similar to anger rising up within you also but it is not anger it is a feeling where suddenly you feel you need to be active and clear and throw things out with a great determination. That is your fire.

There are so many stages upon the spiritual path, stages to self realisation and at each stage you reclaim more of your fire but life will often dampen our fire and we allow that to happen when we are not strong enough to completely own that fire. If you find that you have situations around you in your life where people are being disrespectful to you or they are controlling you or they do not allow you to be fully yourself do not allow yourself to dampen your fire keep it blazing and use your voice which is your fire to speak out to say no.

The fire is in the voice, it is in the heart, it is at the base of the spine and it is also in the third eye for when we have the fire we can see clearly. If you have any problems with your heart or lower back pain or with your eyes then go and tend to your fire and see if you have squashed it or pushed it down by not fully accepting the things that you see.

Unleash your fire and feel it as the colour of fire flowing through every part of you, through your physical body and your emotional body and into your soul. When you have too much water within you and here I'm speaking about the emotional body where you find that you are dealing with many emotions when you bring in the fire it will dry up the water within you so that you are not submerged within the watery realm of the emotions which can be overpowering.

Take your fire now and let it blaze and you will find that you feel more empowered than you have ever felt before, do not give your fire away to others so that there is little left for yourself, claim it completely, set yourself afire with who you truly are and when anyone tries to make you less than you are then blaze even more.

Claiming your fire is claiming your true self.

Memories

Our lives are full of many experiences and many connections and they are all meant to be, every one them and it is these experiences and connections which create the richness of life.

We have a lovely little crystal clock which was given to us as a wedding present and I am often drawn to it and I think of the couple who gave it to us. We have not connected with them for a long time but it is nice to reflect upon our memories.

I met the friend who gave us the clock a long time ago in my home town of South Shields in the north-east. My husband at that time and I had set up a Friends Of The Earth group and we became very interested in the environment and natural ways of healing. I became very drawn to natural ways of eating for healing and I invited a man who ran the East-West Centre in Edinburgh to come and give a talk to our group and to the public about macrobiotics. Macrobiotics is a holistic way of eating by being in tune with the environment, the seasons and with the self.

That talk changed much for me and it was from then that my passion for natural food escalated and I decided to put an advert in the local paper to invite people to join me to discuss this. This was in the days before the Internet so if you wanted to reach out to people then it was done through publications.

An American lady was one of the people who got in touch and we met in a little group in a pub with others and she and I became good friends. She was a very interesting lady and previously she had fled to Italy from America with her two children with Interpol chasing her because of difficulties with her ex-husband. Everything was sorted for her and she found a job as an au pair with an English lady. Then one day the brother of her employer came to visit and the moment he met my friend he fell in love with her.

He returned home and he lived in South Shields but not long after my friend came to England with the children as she had more problems relating to her ex-husband. Everything worked out well for them and it was then that we met up. After a while the two of them went to live in northern Italy and we visited and stayed in their home in the Aosta Valley, a very beautiful place near the Swiss border. They then returned back to the north-east and settled for a little while but one day my friend woke up and she said to the universe that they were going to go and live in Park City. Park City is in the mountains in Utah and without any delay again everything worked out, the house was sold and they relocated to Utah.

Not long after this I was visiting my brother in California at Christmas and he gave me a big box as a Christmas present and inside were other boxes and as I opened them ripping off all the paper I eventually came to a plane ticket with my name on it to Salt Lake City so that I could go and visit my friend. I flew there and stayed with her and her husband up in the mountains in the ski resort of Park City. As a gift to me they had bought me a training session with a skiing instructor. Now I am not sporty, I hated sports at school, give me the hedgerows and the woods and I am happy so you can imagine my dismay at this gift. I spent the day with the ski instructor being totally rubbish at skiing but it was an experience.

I share this story with you to let you know that with everything we do and every person we meet these things are all meant to be and even if some of the people we meet do not stay in our lives there is always a purpose.

I had rich experiences through meeting my friend, experiences which I won't forget and which touch me still so remember that every encounter you make and every experience you have personally is part of the rich tapestry of your life helping you to create your own stories.

The Solar Body

As we move into a golden age we move into a solar
age and we are shifting into solar beings.

We are influenced by both the moon and the sun and
we have both within us, female and male aspects
blended together but it is the moon which rules us
more than anything. The moon is the emotional body
and we are ruled by our emotions and it is the old
emotions within us which keep us trapped and stop us
from moving forward.

We are influenced so much by the moon physically
and mentally and emotionally and just as the tides are
governed by the moon we are too, more than we can
ever begin to understand. You can liken our lunar
body to our physical body here grounded upon the
earth and our solar body as the higher part of us which
holds our wisdom and exists only as light.

We have worked through our lunar bodies for so very
long and now it is time to claim our solar body and by
doing this we can move into a higher state of
consciousness. The ancients knew the secrets of the
solar energies; they worked with the sun and their

bodies would glow with pale golden light because they understood the magic of the solar energy.

The moon feeds our deep intuitive knowing but it also feeds our emotions often making it difficult for us to rise above to see the truth in the full light of understanding. The sun lifts us up into the higher lands of self understanding and a deep awareness of all things.

The golden age is very much in the future, way into the future but it is coming and we are the ones who are preparing the way for all that is to come for harmony and peace upon the planet. As we evolve we will grow into our bodies of light and at this time we are at the very beginning of the slow process of stepping into our solar bodies.

Become more aware than ever of the solar energy and this does not mean that you have to bathe in the sunlight for you can go deep within and find your inner sun and each day bathe in golden showers of sunbeams. Try this daily, enter into your solar plexus, your sun centre and sit beneath a blazing sun and absorb its frequency deep into your being and see what a difference it makes to you. Everything is within us, the whole universe is within and we have access to all that and you can enter through the gateway of your inner knowing and receive many blessings and much light and healing.

By embracing our solar bodies it does not mean that we leave behind our deep intuitive knowing from the lunar aspect of us for that is already incorporated within us but it means we move further into the golden light which is preparing us for the golden path ahead. Work with sunflowers, work with your solar plexus and work with your inner sun and this will bring you healing for your physical body and your emotional body and it will light you up like never before illuminating the way for you as you move forward. Claim your light and claim your sun and maybe you too will radiate a golden glow to shine upon others who are still under the moon.

The Bluebell Temple

Very often when people describe to me their spiritual experiences they will ask me if it was just their imagination as they describe the things they have seen. The imagination is the doorway to spirit and it is through the imagination that we can access the hidden inner mystical worlds. Allow your imagination to run as free as it can and it will bring you back many gifts of wisdom and healing.

There are realms within realms in the world around us and when you enter into the mystic you can enter in to the world of all things whether that is flowers or crystals or trees, you can actually enter into the very essence of all that they represent to receive their teachings and their healing.

At the moment it is the time of the bluebells and they bring their healing colour of blue and they bring so much magic into our lives for there is nothing more magical than a carpet of bluebells and even if you cannot visit the bluebells in person you can go within and receive from them in the same way.

Here is a healing journey for you into the world of the Bluebell.

Go deep within so very deep and just keep going deeper and deeper, deep into the velvety blackness of your inner self.

Eventually you will come to a blue door and when you step through it you will be in the realm of the bluebells. You will see before you a carpet of bluebells in a woodland scene and that carpet will lead you like a path to the Bluebell Temple. When you eventually arrive at the Bluebell Temple you will stand in awe at what you see before you for in front of you is the most beautiful temple made of blue stone and carved upon its pillars are many bluebells.

As you stand before the door you will hear the tinkling of many bells and these are the bells of the bluebells announcing your arrival. You step through the door and you enter into the most beautiful place but it is the energy of this Temple which touches you deeply in the heart for it seems to touch the inner child within you, the child within who remembers the elementals and the fairies, the unseen beings who inhabit our planet. Appearing before you are many beings who come dressed in the colour of the bluebells and they are as light as a feather and they bring to you a greater lightness of being. Their voices sound like the tinkling of water and they surround you with so much love. You gaze around this beautiful temple and you take in its beauty and you notice everything within it. There is so much light in here and it is healing light just for you.

The elementals take you to the healing space within the temple and they ask you to lie down upon a bed of the softest green moss and they come around you holding bells of blue ringing them all around you transforming the energies in your aura.

As they do this you feel any physical pain and any emotional pain being transformed by the sound and the colour of the bells and a great peace fills your being. The Bluebell fairies then begin to sing their Bluebell song and you hear it like a great orchestra of light and that light brings great healing to you.

Let your imagination have wings and let it fly so high opening you to the unlimited realms which wait for you.

The Higher Self

Our higher selves always know what we need and when we listen we can receive continuous guidance as to what is best for us for our higher self always takes care of us, it is our own guardian angel.

Earlier in the week I pulled a muscle in my leg and so I have been hobbling about since then but it is so much better and on the mend now. I understood fully what this meant and it was for me to slow down and just stop and spend more time sitting quietly. It is so fascinating that when we don't listen and hear the call to slow down then the higher self steps in and it will create a situation to make us stop.

I have experienced this time and time again over the years where circumstances have made me stop for a little while because it was time to stand back and be quiet. This happens again continuously upon the spiritual path and people will often ask me why is it that everything has gone quiet, why have the guides all run away and why is nothing happening and I always tell them that this is for a reason.

We are constantly evolving and moving from one level to the next inwardly as we expand our consciousness but there are times where we need to stop and digest all we have learnt and re-evaluate ourselves and our work and our life and then we are ready to move once again into new energy.

This is part and parcel of the spiritual path and so I share this with you so that you too can be aware of when it is time to stop and give time to yourself to take stock of where you are at. It is often during these times where we are able to see in truth where we are at now for we often do not realise how much we have achieved and how much we have grown.

So I have spent more time this week sitting quietly and reflecting and when I have gone to get on with tasks I have felt an old shoulder injury making itself known and even yesterday I felt a twinge in my back so I said okay I will listen.

I find this quite amusing because sometimes we are so determined to push through to continue when the higher self is telling us to stop and stand back and sit. It is only during those times where we can truly listen and hear and listen to the instructions we are being given for our future.

So take notice of when you get that feeling that you need to stand back and listen to your body as well for it will tell you when you need to be less active. This is so much part of the spiritual path I have seen it in myself so many times and I have seen it in others and very often people don't understand what is happening and they get very despondent and down.

I am absolutely fine and my leg is fine but I know I still need more time to digest and to ruminate and to listen and I will know when it is time to be more active.

How wise is the higher self for it knows everything and it looks after us and takes care of us. So listen to your higher self to the subtle messages being brought to you, guiding you and telling you what to do and when those times come where you need to be quiet then go and enjoy it fully and give to yourself and nurture yourself and have no guilt about not getting on with things. This is part of your journey.

A friend asked me the other day how I was getting on and I said to her as long as I can hobble to the fridge to get my wine then I am quite happy.

The Great Central Sun

Many of you will have heard the term, the great
Central Sun and maybe you have your own
interpretation of what this means. Some people
actually think it is a sun and they connect it to different
stars and constellations.

Our own Sun has always been seen by the ancients of
this planet as being the closest they could ever come to
knowing the great divine light from where we all
came. This is why the sun was honoured in most
ancient cultures. The golden light which gave
everything life was the closest anyone could see in
physical manifestation to the light of the divine. The
sun is so important as we are moving into a solar
civilisation and we will begin to remember the ancient
sun healing techniques which were used in the past.
As in all things spiritual now you do not have to
connect to the physical expression of what you are
using for healing all you need to do is to manifest it
with your mind and you can do this by using the sun
for healing. You manifest the sun and the sunlight and
the sun's rays and you fill yourself with this light and
it brings the most incredible healing.

If we talk about the great Central Sun it is not a sun and it is not anywhere in the physical universe, it is a metaphor for the great light, the creative source and the origin of all things. If you look at the ancient texts like the Bhagavad Gita you will read of how the face of Krishna would shine like a million suns and very often the description of the great beings of light who teach us and guide us are seen to have faces which shine like the sun. This is showing us the great light behind everything.

The great Central Sun is the source of all things and you could call it what you wish, god, goddess, divinity, the source. I always like to use the words, the divine, I am not always comfortable using god and I don't like using god without using goddess as well so for me the source is the divine.

The great Central Sun, the source of all things, the divine light is actually within you for you carry a spark of divinity within you, your divine self, for you are not separate and so the great Central Sun is within you. You do not have to travel to it for there is nowhere to go, everything is always within you and the divine light is who you truly are.

Use the sun for healing in your visualisations, put the sun in your solar plexus or on those parts of your body where you have pain, bring in the sunflower and use it for healing and plant that in your solar plexus as well. Also go within to the source, the spark of the great light and find your own great Central Sun within you for it does indeed reside within you.

The light of our own Sun is only just the tiniest fraction of the light of the great Central Sun and even then we couldn't even begin with our limited minds to understand the magnitude of that light. Go within and find your own Central Sun and know that it is a spark of the source which you carry within you for you do indeed carry the great Central Sun inside you. Enter into it and find the bliss and the healing which waits for you.

Bhakti

When I first began my spiritual journey in earnest I
began with Hinduism not with the religion but with
the spiritual aspect of it, the meditation, the chanting
and the many books which I read. It fitted me so well
and in the years to come where I have studied many
different types of spirituality it was always Hinduism
which brought me back home. To me it was home.
It resonated so deeply within me and it touched
something that I could never put into words and the
only way I can describe it is that one of the most
beautiful aspects of Hinduism is something called
bhakti. Bhakti means devotion.
I had been brought up a Roman Catholic and even
though it did incredible damage to me emotionally and
much had to be undone the seeds of devotion were
planted within me from a very early age. The devotion
of bhakti is indescribable, it does not mean devotion to
any deity or anyone it is a vibration, a feeling in the
heart, a feeling of the knowledge of the unity of all
things and of the light which is the love behind all
things. It can only be experienced it cannot be learnt

for it is a direct connection to something which is beyond words.

It is a strange thing that many people who are drawn to my work also have this deep connection to Hinduism and to India, they feel the pull very strongly and even though those who come to me for the teachings and they receive the teachings of mother Earth and the magic of the earth there is often that same magnetic pull within them.

I remember many years ago being told that the foundation of my work was Taoism but the vibration of it was Krishna. I understood what this meant which was that the foundation of all I teach comes from the mysteries of the earth but the vibration which runs through it all is that of Hinduism.

Upon the spiritual path we bow to no-one, we learn to be empowered and we bow to no deities and ascended beings we see them as equal for the time has gone where we look up to those who we think know better than we do. We have god goddess within and we have unlimited wisdom within and we are part of the whole.

Nature is my church but I have a Hindu heart. Namaste.

Mystical Realms

They are worlds within worlds, right here, right now where we are, for we live in a multi dimensional state. We are multi dimensional and so is existence. If we could truly see we would see the many layers of being which exist all around us but these are kept hidden from us however we can enter deep within and access the doorways and the portals to the mystical worlds which are present now.

There is nowhere to go, nowhere to reach, nowhere to ascend to there is only the going within to access deeper mystical states. There are many stories of Shangri-La, Camelot, Avalon and many more, mystical worlds filled with beauty and peace and harmony. These worlds exist on a different plane of consciousness and we can discover them and enter within.

I often use as a key or a doorway mist for mist is a symbol of the mystical and there are many stories also of people entering special places as they travelled through the mist. You too can call in the mist and make your intention to travel to the mystical realms which are part of everything here now.

Let me take you on a journey so that you can see for yourself the beauty which is already here for you. You may tell yourself that what you see is only your imagination but your imagination is also a gateway to the hidden realms, it is so important so allow your imagination free rein and it will enable you to enter the realms of beauty.

Sit quietly and call in the mist and feel it wrap around you with a softness and gentleness and sit within this mist and go deep within yourself, go so deep, deeper than you have ever been before. After a little while the mists will part and you will find yourself looking upon the most glorious landscape. It will look very much like the earth but you will immediately realise that it carries a different quality for everything looks as though it is made of the most beautiful vibrant light. You will see the same trees and flowers and landscape but they will be lit up and not only will it be the light which sets it apart from our everyday reality it is the feeling more than anything which will show you that you have entered another realm. The feeling will hit you in the heart for it will be full of love and peace and harmony.

You will meet beings here, beings in a human body but with a difference for they too are made of luminous light and also they will be filled with peace and love and harmony. Let them reveal to you the mysteries in this world remembering that this is also a part of our world it is just that we cannot normally see it.

Allow your companions to teach you about this world and as they do you will find that you fill up with the luminous radiant light of many colours and so that when it is time to return you will bring that light back with you and it will fill you and nourish you and heal you. When it is time to leave this place call in the mist again and when it clears you will be back in your everyday reality but you will have the knowledge that you can return to the hidden realms at any time you wish. Magic is real, it exists and there is magic here now and you have within you many dimensions of yourself and many dimensions of reality which you can access too so enter the mist, the mystical and find the magic which waits for you.

Listen

I love stories and here is one for you.

A couple of days ago a bee had been buzzing around me and I knew it was my mother as that is one of her symbols, she had been given the title of Queen Bee once upon a time. I must add that she hated that title. In the afternoon I sat on the swing seat and a bee came around me again and I said okay, "Mam, send me a sign that you are here". I immediately jumped up from the seat and came inside and turned on the computer and there was a message from my dear friend Jenny. Included in the message was a picture of my mother. Jenny had just received my brother's autobiography and when she opened the book it was on the page with a picture of my mother on her hundredth birthday and Jenny had taken a photograph of it to send to me.

I am sure that my Mam had whispered in Jenny's ear that day because no sooner had I asked for a sign then there it was.

There is magic everywhere so connect to it and always ask and ask your loved ones in spirit to send you a sign too to show you that they are with you

Mam

When we look back at all the events and people from our lives we sometimes tend to reflect more on the things which caused us pain rather than on the things which brought us joy but on the path of healing you eventually come to a place where you can look upon both sides of the situation and you see it in wholeness and completeness.

Today I mentioned something to Graham, my husband, about my mother and as soon as I did my heart just burst open with love for her. She has been gone now 11 years and she had been one of my greatest teachers in many ways. She had four breakdowns in her life and she was a very emotional person and so I learnt how to worry and be anxious like she was but it was those very things which gave us both deep sensitivity and awareness of others. When I felt that overwhelming love today it came as a great surprise and I was flooded with the love for her and all that she was and all that she gave to me. She was an amazing woman who throughout her hundred and one years was as feisty and demanding until the end.

I share this with you so that you too may look back and see both sides of things and that will bring you inner peace. My mother or my Mam as I always called her left home at 16 and she worked in hotels as a waitress or she worked as a housekeeper until she met my Dad when she was 29.

She told me many tales of when she worked at the Kensington Hotel in London and of the many friends she made there. People think that in the olden days there wasn't as much fun but believe me my mother knew how to have fun.

She had many sisters; they were known as the Maguire sisters by everyone and they had a wonderful reputation for where ever they went there was always much laughter. They travelled abroad together visiting all the holy places and having the time of their lives. They would all congregate at our house on Monday nights and the laughter could be heard halfway down the road, they always laughed even when they were dealing with difficult situations.

It is a strange thing that my sister became friends with the daughter of the lady who had been my Mam's best friend when they were young and they are the greatest of friends now.

My Mam would tell the story of how she and her friend got drunk in the pantry on Sherry when they were teenagers. She had a wonderful time as a teenager going to parties and I remember she told me that she and her friends would hire a house for the day for a party.

As they got older and their friends passed on they loved to go to the funerals of everyone and even in their sorrow they had a very sociable time. On one occasion they were bought that much whiskey my Auntie Maureen had to be carried out of the pub into the taxi. They would all go out together with their husbands to nightclubs and there were times where they would sneak in some drink in their handbags. There were so many stories to be told and so many characters in the family we still laugh about those stories today. It has been my Dad around mainly recently but I'm sure that my Mam is here today for me to have so many memories and to feel so much love for her. As I reflected upon this I thought if I had been working in the Kensington Hotel at the same time as she was I am sure we would have been great friends for we loved the same things.

I can feel her smiling and I feel more love for her for who she was than ever before. So look back and reflect and see two sides of the story of everything and when you find the love the greatest healing takes place

Mary Magdalene

People often think that Mary Magdalene came from
Magdala and that is why she is called Magdalene. It is
more than likely that she came from Capernaum and
the name Magdalene given to her meant tower.
Mary was given the name of the tower because she
was a tower of strength and she towered above many
others. Her presence and her essence in the world
today is to enable us to become a tower of strength for
ourselves no longer hiding in the shadows but being
fully embodied in our own god and goddess self.
When you make the decision to stand in your full
empowerment and in your true self you become a
Magdalene, you become a tower of strength and so
you carry the essence of all that she represents within
yourself. There are many Magdalenes in the world
now inspired by all that she stands for and they shine
their light onto others helping them and teaching them
to become their own Magdalenes.
So if you call yourself a Magdalene you are recognising
that you have stepped into your own sovereignty so
that you are king or queen of your own realm, your
own universe, your own self and your beingness

comes from the god and goddess within. To be a
Magdalene is to speak your truth, to accept that you
have the power within you to be whatever you want to
be and to do what ever you want to do and that you do
not need anyone else to approve of you.

If you are practising coming further into the light and
standing up for yourself and being strong and not
wavering in what you believe then you are well on
your way to sovereignty and you are well on your way
to becoming a Magdalene. There are so many
struggling still too afraid to be themselves but there is
help and the light glimmers through the cracks of the
old world revealing that it is possible to just be you.

In her lifetime Magdalene spoke out and she spoke out
particularly to the women who were her followers and
she spoke the truth and others saw this in her and they
saw that she was a tower of strength and they were
afraid of the power within her. History treated her
cruelly or should I say the Catholic Church treated her
cruelly by telling the lies about her and this was all in
the name of denigrating women and taking away their
power.

Even if you have memories in this lifetime of lives
where your power was taken from you you do not
have to go back into other lives all you need to do is to
be who you are in your full light in this life and say to

yourself, I am the tower. Become Magdalenes and shine your light for everyone to see and speak your truth and if others do not like it that is their problem not yours.

If you haven't yet reclaimed your full power then take back every bit of it now, stand tall and you too can be a tower of strength not only for yourself but for others also.

The Cave Of Eggs

Yesterday was the first day of spring, the spring equinox, Ostara and there are many symbols associated with this time of new beginnings. One of the most potent symbols is the egg and the symbolism of the egg has been held sacred since ancient times. Above the cave where Mary Magdalene lived in the latter part of her life on the St. Baume Mountain in Provence in France is another cave higher up and this cave is called the Cave Of Eggs because there are egg - like structures within the stone. On the side of Glastonbury Tor is the Egg Stone, again a huge egg - shaped stone. Both the Cave Of Eggs and the Egg Stone on the Tor are very sacred places.

We all know that the egg means new beginnings and this is the time of new beginnings where we plant new seeds both within and without and we watch as the first stirrings of new life take place not only upon mother Earth but within ourselves for we have the cycle of the seasons within us. We constantly move from winter into spring and the whole cycle begins again when we come out of the shadows and into the light, the light of ourselves and of true understanding.

We are like the egg for we have been conditioned by the things we have been taught since childhood and the path to healing is about undoing that conditioning, healing is all about undoing. We have created shells around ourselves as protection for when you are vulnerable you need to preserve yourself. This is not protection as taught by some spiritual people where you need to surround yourself with light out of fear this is about keeping safe our inner light.

There comes a time when you don't need that shell any more and the first cracks let in the light so that you see the light, you see the truth and you realise that you do not need to hide any more. Many of us have hidden in past lives out of fear of persecution and as healers and spiritual people we have lived in times where it was not safe to reveal our true selves. Then in this present life many of you will have had relationships and situations in your life where you were afraid to totally reveal yourself out of fear of condemnation or anger or being dismissed for what you believe but you cannot live like that anymore.

When you see the symbolism of an egg shell cracking and you say, I have cracked it, you have got the understanding so it is time now to let any shell around you crack so that you can be revealed in your full light and you can be seen by everyone and when we are seen we speak our truth without any fear.

Take yourself to the Cave Of Eggs, the cave above Magdalene's Cave on the mountain and sit in that cave amongst the egg stones there and see yourself being encased in a shell and let the energy of this sacred place enable you to push outwards so that you can emerge from your shell and into the light. The cave represents the womb and very often we are symbolically in the womb in winter time where we are safe but the time comes when you cannot stay hidden any more.

After you have cracked your shell gather it up, all the pieces of it and see the truth of it that it is only what you created to keep your light safe so take that shell, gather it in your hands and blend it together so that it becomes fertiliser for the new you and sprinkle this around your roots which are your feet and feel yourself ready now to grow into the new you.

Step out of the cave and see how high up you are and look out over the Provencal landscape and you will be able to see for miles for when you come out of your shell you see everything with crystal clarity

The Spark

Did you know that you have unlimited healing within yourself and for yourself. You have all the power of the creative force within you to create healing. You carry a spark of divinity within you and you are part of the whole creative source of all things and when you connect in to that creative source you connect to the unlimited power of healing.

There is a force within you which is intelligent and you can communicate with it and you can instruct it to heal your body and in that way you become the master of your physical self. How many times do you put yourself down and speak in negative ways about yourself whether it is on the physical or the emotional level and your body listens to you and it will confirm for you your thoughts. However if you give your body positive thoughts then it will confirm these for you and create healing.

Talk to your body, talk to your cells and tell them that you are in charge and that they are healthy and healed and filled with light and the life force. Give yourself and your body instructions to create whatever healing you wish for. Feed your body positive thoughts every day of your life.

This is different from positive thinking, this is actually taking control and being in command and saying what you want and speaking of it in the present here now as if it has already happened. So for instance you wouldn't ask for healing for a certain part of your body you would speak as though it was already healed and bursting with health. Once you confront the cells or even the atoms or the DNA of your body it is as though they wake up and like little children they are ready to take the initiative from you and if you tell them they are healthy then that is what they will believe.

In the future healing will be done completely in this way without any need for any of the ways which we heal with at the moment even though all those wonderful ways of healing are tremendous but in the future it will all be done with the mind and we are seeing the beginning of this way of working now in the present time. You will tell your body to heal, you will speak of it as though it is already healed and every day you will tell it that it is bursting with new life and good health.

When you see yourself as part of the creative force you then begin to slowly understand that you are in charge for you are the creator yourself. You are god goddess, you are divine and because of this you can create with your intentions, with your mind. Start today and speak to your body at the cellular level or speak to your organs or bodily systems and command them to upgrade to good health and well-being and speak of these parts of you as being vibrant with healing and light. Mean every word that you say and practice it so that it becomes a daily ritual and if you find yourself at any time speaking negatively about your body or yourself then just stop and take a moment to reflect and know that your body is listening.

Your body listens and it takes instructions from you so now give it good instructions and watch how you thrive and the angels of healing will surround you for they wait in unlimited numbers to support you and when they hear that you have changed your way of thinking and have taken charge and that you are not at the mercy of your body, you are its leader, they will surround you with even more light.

Take charge and speak in the most positive terms and healing will be yours and speak of it as though it has already been accomplished

Avalon

Last September Graham and I were very fortunate to visit Glastonbury and while we were there we went into the Abbey which is such a glorious place. The ruins are amazing but so is the land there and my favourite place of all is the orchard.

The apple trees were laden with fruit and there were many windfalls on the ground so we picked up three and brought them back home with us. It felt so special to have these apples from Avalon whose name means land of apples and I planted the seeds and now six months later one seed has germinated. I have watched and waited for this to happen and I was absolutely overjoyed to see this and I'm sure that the others will germinate as well.

So we have a little bit of Glastonbury Abbey here in our garden but the truth is Glastonbury is here where we are in this moment for Glastonbury is the heart. I love Glastonbury and I have visited many times and I always feel the same when I return. When we travel down the M5 and I see the turnoff for Glastonbury I always feel as though I'm going home and then as you approach the town and you see the Tor it is always a thrill.

There are many orchards on the slopes of the Tor and they are all special and they carry the most wonderful energy. Some years ago the Magdalene Priestesses who had trained with me were initiated in the orchard at Middlewick just outside Glastonbury. We held our ceremony in the orchard with mistletoe on the trees and the Tor in the background and Jenny sang for us and we danced around the apple trees. What a glorious day it was in the land of the goddess.

If you cut an apple in half horizontally it reveals the mark of the goddess within it, the five pointed star which it carries at its heart. Apples are so magical and mystical and they connect us to the land of apples, to Glastonbury, so take yourself there for healing and sit in the orchard amongst the apple blossom.

Sit under the apple trees in the orchard in the Abbey and feel the sacred soil beneath your feet, feel the goddess who is in every part of the landscape here and let her come to you and bring you a crystal chalice filled with golden apple juice and drink deeply from it and let it bring you healing for body and mind.

The symbol of the apple represents wisdom and its golden juice again brings the gold of wisdom so take this gift of the cup of gold and rest awhile in the warm sun amongst the blossoms of the trees and listen to the buzzing of the bees as they go about their work. Let this sacred landscape heal you and bring you peace in the heart for Glastonbury is the heart centre of the world and its apples are the sacred fruits of divine wisdom.

Magic

I have just been looking through some pictures and quite by chance I came across one of our wedding day and I don't know the reason why but I am being guided to share this with you.

It was a picture of our wedding day in 1998 when we ran away to Gretna Green. Graham and I have both been married before and so we just wanted a quiet time.

It was a wonderful day and after this we honeymooned in the Lake District and then we travelled across the country to South Shields to stay with my mother.

My mother had organised a wedding feast for us at a local hotel and family and friends were invited. As we all sat down to dinner the most amazing thing happened because as the chef came out of the kitchen carrying a dish I couldn't believe what I was seeing.

It was my brother in a chef's hat, my brother whom I thought was in California where he lives and he had come over specially to be present and he brought his family. My brother Michael loves a joke and he loved making people happy and he had organised this for

Graham and I and it was the most wonderful occasion ever.

During the afternoon as he checked into the hotel my cousin was taking a wedding cake into the restaurant and she actually saw him but she never said a word. So Graham and I had a wonderful wedding first of all at Gretna Green where I had roses in my hair and bluebells from the garden in my bouquet. During our honeymoon I said to Graham find me a bluebell wood and indeed he did in Whitemoss Common at Rydal Water and we took pictures in a sea of bluebells.

Our memories and our stories carry magic within them and when we tell them a little bit of the magic finds its way to others. May there always be a little bit of magic in your life as well.

Shamrock

My dad came to a friend recently and he gave her a shamrock to give to me. He has been very much around me and I would like to share the shamrock with you. He always brings the green with his Irish heritage and the green of nature which he loved and he shares the shamrock with you for it is the most wonderful healer when you place it in your heart and allow its vibration and its colour to fill you.

I was brought up a Catholic and every Saint Patrick's day we would receive a box from Ireland containing shamrock. It was sent to us by two of my dad's sisters, Nora and Cis, two beautiful gentle ladies who wore black for the rest of their lives after bereavements in the family.

We would wear the shamrock on Saint Patrick's Day and then at school which was a Catholic convent school there was always a performance of Irish dancing from some of the girls.

Quite a number of years ago a friend of mine who loved to visit a convent here on the Wirral would collect shamrock from there and one time she left some on my doorstep and it took root and I planted it in the garden. From that time every year shamrock grows and seeds everywhere.

This beautiful plant carries the threefold symbolism which is inherent in all spirituality, the three aspects of the goddess and of the divine and when we bring this in we bring the union of body, mind and spirit within us too. The shape of a plant or flower is very important in revealing its healing medicine but the colour is its greatest attribute.

Green is the colour for the heart and the deeper the green the deeper the healing which takes place so bring in the shamrock and let its light and its vibration fill you completely, let its colour flow through every part of your being and then sit within the green. There is a term called the Greening but in spiritual understanding it is about the Greening of ourselves, the coming to the heartland of who we truly are.

Wear the green, eat green vegetables and take in the green of the landscape, take in the green of the shamrock and remember that Ireland is not called the Emerald Isle for nothing for the Emerald is the stone of the heart.

There is such a strong feeling at the moment of the ancient green tracks and ancient green places and they can bring you much solace and healing if you go there in your inner journeying. You can go to meet the

Druids, the gods and goddesses and the elemental beings. Bring in the green for it brings in mother nature in all her glory and sit within this colour and let the peace and the calmness of it completely fill you.

Merlin

This week the energy of Merlin has been very apparent and when I speak of Merlin you can interpret that in any way, either as the being whom we know as Merlin or as the Merlin energy which is the essence of magic and transformation.

There are two energies we work with, there is an earthly energy and a spiritual energy and they both need to be in balance but there are times where one or the other will be more dominant depending on what is going on within your life. However spiritual energy is positive energy for it is the creative source of everything.

The Merlin energy is very positive for it brings magic and all magic is is transformation and when we use our minds in a positive way we could transform anything; that is the magic. We are attuned to the creative force and we are a channel for it, it is always there, it always has been and it always will be.

You can call this creative force what ever you choose, you can call it god or goddess or the divine or the source but it is there without form and we have access to it at any time. When we are very creative and inspired we are actually using this energy and some people may call it ascension energy for it is the energy of creativity from the creator, the creative source of all things. Remember that you are also the creator.

When we are aligned to positive energy we are using the energy of the Merlin, the energy of change and transformation. I am sure you have had many experiences where you have felt down or immersed in negative energy and you have used your mind to change your vibration instantly by bringing in the positive. We need to be in what we would call negative energy at times for that is where our deepest teachings and wisdom come from, the deepest teachings of all do not come from the positive they come from the negative for it is only in the dark, the darkness of the mind when it isn't in the light that we can truly feel and see the truth of all things.

When we send healing to someone we are channelling the creative force sending it to another person. There was a beautiful experience the other night in a group I was holding where one of the ladies received the energy and she sent it on to her friend and this is how it works, we receive it, we channel it through us and we send it out to someone and maybe that person will send it out yet again. Be aware every day that you are attuned to the creative force, the positive energy, the light of healing and you have access to it constantly. Use this positive energy and use the magic of the Merlin every day. Clear your energy body; create magic in all sorts of ways by letting the light transform any stuck energy within you. There are so many ways you can do this. Use your magic and use your mind to create change by working with the light in whichever way you are drawn to do.

Go and find yourself a wand if you do not have one but never break off a branch from the tree always take your wand from a gift of a branch which has fallen to the ground and bring it home and make some magic. Create a golden circle with your wand and stand within it and draw down the heavenly light and let it wash through you like heavenly waters and wash out any old energy which you are holding onto and feel the emotions within it. Then step out of the circle and with your wand transform everything you have released into something filled with colour and light and put it back in your aura so that you are filled with colour and light.

Then when you have finished say the words and so it is. Remember always use words which indicate that whatever you are intending has already been accomplished.

My Dad

Whenever I need a tonic my dad comes to me and he brings me the deepest green colour. Sometimes I share remedies from him and I call him Uncle Tom because my numerous cousins called him that while others in the family called him Dr. Quack because he always had a remedy for everything. He knew the country ways from his life in Cork in Ireland and from his father who was a gardener.

What a wonderful man my dad was and I was brought up on the joys of nature and the magic inherent in nature and the elementals. He brings the deepest darkest green for you because he knows that many of you need a tonic at this time and this tonic will help you emotionally and physically for it is for body and mind.

He brings it to you in a little crystal bottle and he asks that you just take one drop at a time then sit and let this magical liquid flow through every part of you. The deepest darkest green has the most powerful magic within it, it is so special. It is like having all the green from nature blended together to make an elixir of life just for you.

My dad has been present recently and it is such a comfort to have him around me and he has often come through the years and through other people to bring me messages and guidance. I love it when he comes. Your own ancestors come to you as well and even when you think there is no one around you in spirit they are still there looking after you even if it is sometimes from a distance. When our ancestors come very often they bring comfort and reassurance; that is one of their primary jobs and if you need comfort and reassurance sit quietly and feel in the space around you who is there with you.

One of the ways that I know my dad is around is when Graham will say to me, I'm just resting my eyes. That was one of my dad's favourite sayings so we know we have company when we hear words and sayings which those who have passed over would often speak. They try so hard at times to let us know that they are there.

People go to mediums not only for guidance but for reassurance that they are not alone and that those they have loved haven't gone anywhere.

The work of the medium is to bring through relatives who have passed over and it is such a wonderful job for it is not enough just to have trust and faith for we are human as well and our humanity requires as much attention as our spiritual selves.

Just know that you are never alone, there is always someone around you and today my dad brings you some help with this tonic of the deepest green in the crystal bottle for he sees how much it is needed by many of you.

Stories

I always tell stories and I love to listen to the stories of other people and it is through stories that we can learn so much. In my mother's later years when I would visit her we would sit around the fire drinking whiskey and she would reminisce about her life and I would love to hear about her experiences and much laughter was shared and these memories are precious.

I often write tales about my own life for there are always teachings in our experiences. In days gone by the storyteller would journey from village to village and even today there are professional storytellers, stories are so important.

In my early life when I was at school and a student I had several jobs, I was a post lady, I did stocktaking at Woolworths, I worked in a dry cleaners and I was a chalet maid at Butlins in Skegness one summer but after I left college I became an infant teacher. I did not really want to be a teacher but the convent school I went to encouraged only three choices of nursing, teacher training or university. I even went to see a careers' advisor outside of school for some guidance and the only guidance I was given was to join the Wrens, some chance of that.

In the end I went to a teacher training college in Liverpool because my friends were going and we all chose to study art there. They were very happy days and when I eventually began to teach I loved the children but for me the most important part of each day in school was story time.

The last session of the day was devoted to stories and in midwinter I would turn off the lights and tell scary stories to the children which they absolutely adored. There were many wonderful fairy stories as well and we would sit together cosily enjoying that special time but I always had to make sure that the naughty ones sat cross-legged at my feet.

My first year of teaching was in a place called Kirkby on the outskirts of Liverpool and I was told that if you could teach there you could teach anywhere and so I was given a good grounding for my career. The children loved stories, all children love stories but stories are so important to us as adults and it is so important that we share our stories with one another, there is much to be learnt and much humour also to be gained from them.

As I reflected upon this subject of storytelling I was reminded of a funny story from a few years back when

Graham and I visited my brother in West Palm Beach in Florida. My brother and his partner took us to a famous cafe there called Sprinkles and they had had many famous customers, one of the most famous was John Lennon. As the four of us sat outside we were joined at another table by a couple from Europe and Graham started talking to them. My brother, his partner and Graham then decided to go inside the cafe to read all the posters about all the famous people who came here.

I was sitting on my own outside and the couple reached over to me and said, "We believe that you were a nanny to John Lennon's son Julian." This took me by surprise but then I remembered that Graham's father's cousin was actually a nanny to Cynthia Lennon and so I deducted that he had shared the story with this couple. Thinking quickly I deducted also that this couple had misunderstood Graham and they thought that I was the nanny. Not wanting to deny what Graham had told them I said yes I was the nanny.

What followed was a barrage of questions about John Lennon and I have to admit that I told little white lies as I made things up about being a nanny. As soon as the others came out of the cafe I hurried them down the street and I couldn't stop laughing and no harm was done. When we tell stories we often stretch the truth and embellish our stories to make them more enjoyable and so there is truth in them but also a bit of artistic licence.

I share all this with you to encourage you to share your stories, share the stories of your life, those things that you have experienced and ask others to share their stories with you. If you are still fortunate to have parents encourage them to tell you about their lives when they were younger so that you have a legacy of knowledgeable memories.

Before there were books there were only stories so let us return now to creating much magic in our storytelling as we remember this wonderful art when people sat around the fire and listened in awe to all that was shared with them and if you too indulge in artistic licence then so much the better.

Imbolc

Tomorrow is Imbolc and it is the time of the first spring. Brigid is the goddess of Imbolc and she brings her many blessings to you but her greatest gift is the gift of her eternal flame. The goddess Brigid was blended with Saint Brigid and the stories became intermingled but her essence is always that of bringing us the fire and many need the fire at this time of the year and even though we are still in winter, tomorrow brings the first spring, the first light of new beginnings. Brigid's symbol is the snowdrop, the eternal symbol of hope and when we bring the snowdrop to us it reminds us that even when we are in a long winter of the self we can always bloom and blossom. Our back garden is filled with snowdrops, they were here when we arrived and I remember one year not long after we came here where I posted snowdrop flowers out to people whom I was drawn to send them to. It turned out that each person had a connection with the snowdrop connecting them to a loved one and so they received a healing.

Connect to the snowdrop and even just thinking about it will bring you hope and connect to Brigid; let her come to you dressed in green and she will bring her sacred flame in her hands and she will place it in your heart bringing you the fire to heal and renew yourself. There are times where our fire burns low and literally you feel as though you need to come back to life or you feel tired and weary and it is then where the fire can bring new life and warmth into your being.

The eternal flame burns in Kildare in Ireland as it has done for a long time and it is a reminder of the fire which burns within us always there to connect us to the truth of all things. Fire is life, it is renewal but it is also spirit and the divine fire within you, the spark of divinity which was present from the moment you were conceived and it will be present until the moment you leave this earthly plane and it is always within.

Call upon Brigid today and receive her fire, sit with her amongst the snowdrops or go to the sacred well at Kildare and let her bring you comfort and healing. Her sacred snowdrops are like little lanterns showing us the way so at this time which is also known as Candlemas it is the time of the light and the time to bring in the light. When ever you need lifting up bring in the light and we often forget to do this but it can work miracles bringing the light into the dark so that you can see your way forward.

The light and the fire are the same, they will always bring you back to yourself and bring you comfort and warmth and reconnection so celebrate Imbolc, light your candles and light your fires and bring the fire within then manifest a bunch of snowdrops in your hands and let them fill you with hope eternal.

Sovereignty

The path to wholeness is the path to the self and when you find your self you come home and you claim all the lost parts of you that you have given away throughout your life. This is the healing journey but the healing never stops for it is a continuous spiral forever moving into more unity with the true self. For many of you reading this you will have given yourself away, given away your light on many occasions throughout your life, you will have given your power away but as you journey back to the self you come back to autonomy and sovereignty so that you are in charge of your own domain. When you begin this journey back to wholeness each step is a achievement when you learn to say no, when you learn to speak your truth and when you learn to listen to your voice and not someone else's.

It is a long journey and one which cannot be achieved overnight for it takes years just as it has taken years to strip you of your sense of yourself. Many people have done this to you because you let them as you did not have the understanding or the strength to deny them but as you have grown you have spiralled forward in wholeness. Even when you reach a certain stage and you feel in control of your life there will still be lessons for you to learn for we only ever go deeper into those things which we need to heal.

At the beginning of the journey you attract to you people and situations to test you and sometimes you become overwhelmed by the testing but as time goes on these become fewer and fewer. We only ever draw to us lessons that we need to still learn and if you still draw a lesson to you with the same pattern as previous lessons then know without a doubt whatever it is within you still needs healing. Like attracts like, it is a law of the universe.

Stop for a moment and reassess where you are and give yourself credit for how far you have come to stand in your own power and sovereignty, do not see those times where you have not been able to speak up, look at those times when you have spoken out and spoken back. See how far you have come but know that there is even more for you as you become stronger within and you find your voice and you are not afraid to use it.

I have had to learn this and I am still learning and practically everybody that I teach is still learning the same lesson for it seems to be a universal lesson for us all and particularly for those of us on the spiritual path.

Take back your crown, be King or Queen of your land and don't let anyone ever again take too much from you or deny you your voice. Do not be afraid to use your voice, speak out loud and clear even though you may be quaking in your boots. Own your voice for that is your sovereignty.

Ascension is not some airy fairy notion it is solid and grounded, it is not about ascending somewhere or always being in the light it is about embracing the darkness with the light and finding your way home to yourself. You claim your fears even though they may still be a big part of your life, you claim yourself and you begin to love yourself and you finally understand that you have a right to be heard.

Be in your sovereignty now, be in your own power now and feel what it is like to completely listen to yourself and trust what you hear and to speak your truth and do not waver and do not falter and do not let anyone tell you that you are not right. Wear your crown and rule your land with love first of all for yourself as you stand strong and you become a good and benevolent ruler who understands true sovereignty.

Rue

I would like to share something with you which came into my work the other evening and it was the herb rue. The yellow flower of rue was placed in a chalice of water and this was used as a blessing. This was all done with the light.

This old herb was actually used to make holy water a very long time ago and the herbs would be dipped in the water and sprinkled over people as a blessing.

A blessing is a gift and it is like grace. The meaning of grace is a gift and it is something which is given freely without you having to do anything to receive it.

A blessing bestows upon you the most wonderful energy for positivity and good things so sit quietly and visualise this yellow flower in a chalice of water and sprinkle the water over you and at the same time bless yourself through the words you speak.

You can bless yourself so give this to yourself and sit within the energy and after you have done this let the vibrations of grace flow through you.

Blessed be

Be Yourself

My beloved green wellies stand at our back door and I use them constantly as I go in and out to the garden in summer and winter and when I go out walking when it is wet. Unfortunately they have sprung a leak and as I couldn't go to the shops to buy new ones I have had to order some online and so I have to wait until they arrive.

I wanted to walk down the lanes and so I came up with an idea of putting a plastic bag inside one of them to stop it getting wet. It was a very cold day and so I wore for the first time a crochet hippie hat I had bought recently for the cold weather. As I walked I smiled because I thought I have become a bag lady. I remembered the poem which people spoke of a long time ago about when you grow old you will wear purple well I have worn purple for as long as I can remember and I haven't had to wait until I have grown old to do as I please.

It made me laugh to see the state of me but it was a feeling of joy to think that I could go out with a plastic bag wrapped around my foot and just be me. I hear people saying how they have left their wild side behind as they have grown older but there is no need to do that it is only life's circumstances and the controlling actions of others which make us suppress that part of us which is naughty and free and wild.

I will often say to Graham that I am a disgraceful pensioner in the things that I do but that is absolutely fine. If you feel that you have left the wild side of you in your past then bring it back and embrace it and find the fun in being naughty and outrageous.

Dance naked in the moonlight, talk to yourself as I do when you are out walking, do all manner of things which are out of character and you will find that you return to yourself. Go out roaming and pick the wildflowers and wear your wellies and discover those things within which have been put aside for so long.

I work with the flowers in all my work and when I work with roses if I need to bring in a wild rose I know without a doubt it is because the person I am working with needs to reclaim their wild side. Wild roses are a step further than cultivated roses when you work with them for healing for they are wild and free. Wild roses to me are the epitome of our wildness, our natural side, the part of us which dares to be naughty and shocking and natural.

Call upon a Wild rose now to come and be a mentor for you to teach you how to be you and how to be wild and free. Freedom is a state of mind and the greatest freedom is the freedom to be you but we need to express this on the physical plane and to find the enjoyment and the humour in doing things out of the norm. Become the wild rose and find your freedom, find your naughtiness and you will find that when you reclaim this part of you the echoes of it will reverberate through everything in your life bringing you an even greater sense of yourself.

The 12 Pointed Star

I have already written about the 12 pointed star in the January Magdalene Newsletter and this 12 pointed star is very important at this time for it is one of the symbols of the vibrations of this new year.

We work with different stars in our healing and awakening work and each star carries its own particular energy and its own healing. The five pointed star is a symbol of the divine feminine and it is the star of the rose while the six pointed star is a symbol of the divine masculine and the lily.

Many flowers carry the mark of the star within their geometry and it is fascinating to see this blending of heaven and earth with the star as part of the structure of the flower. We know that the five pointed star amplifies energy and this is why it has been used by the ancients in architecture. If you meditate inside a five pointed star then it will expand your energy. It is the star used in magic and it is also the star of the five elements, the foundation of much healing knowledge. I was shown the 12 pointed star and I included it in a healing journey in my newsletter but this star has remained with me and I would like to share it with you again today so that you can use it for your own healing. The number three carries much wisdom and its vibration and the three has always been used to describe the unified nature of all things and so within the 12 we have four times the three amplifying the power of the three.

The 12 pointed star also carries two six pointed stars within it and so you can understand how powerful it is with the doubling of the potency of the six pointed star.

There is much mystery within the 12 pointed star, there are teachings also but here for you is a way you can use it to bring its essence in so that you are immersed in the new energies for this time and also you can use it for your own personal healing and it will bring you very powerful healing indeed.

Here is a simple way to use the 12 pointed star for healing. Visualise yourself within it and you can imagine that the outer shape of the star is made of any substance, it can be starlight, diamond, gold, silver, you will know what to use. You are to see yourself standing at the very centre of the star for the central point of any star is where its qualities are most powerful. The next part of this healing is up to you for what you are to do is to visualise within each of the 12 points 12 different energies and these 12 different energies will bring you tremendous healing far more powerful than just using one energy.

In each point of the star here is what you can visualise, either 12 great spiritual teachers for they each represent a certain quality of healing, 12 flowers, flowers are very sacred and they can heal you in ways which you could never imagine. You can visualise a crystal in each of the points or you can visualise a colour.

As you stand at the central point within the 12 pointed star with the 12 energies within each of the points with your mind call these energies in to the centre and allow them to fill you completely. You will feel this entering in to your energy and it will feel like electricity and you will receive the vibration of any of the things I have mentioned above and it will be a combination of the 12 vibrations and you are to absorb these energies feeling the star all around you and remember the geometry of the star is part of the important healing aspect of this.

Feel the vibrations flow into you and blend as one and then feel the power of the geometry of the 12 pointed star filling you with its deeply mystical energy. Whenever we work with a star or starlight we are bringing heaven to earth and we bring unity within.

Enjoy this healing and sit quietly after you have accomplished it because it will permeate through all your bodies and bring you renewal, awakening and deep healing.

The Butterfly

On the path of healing we are continually renewing ourselves and one of the most beautiful symbols of renewal and rebirth is the butterfly which also happens to be a symbol of the soul and the heart.

If you feel the need for renewal to renew your energies or if you have been going through a challenging or healing time then here is a journey of rebirth for you. See yourself standing outside at night under a navy blue sky filled with countless shining stars and you look up in wonder at the vision before you. As you gaze into the sky you feel yourself shifting in consciousness from one level of awareness to another and you begin to rise up into the sky.

You rise so high and then you hang suspended looking down in awe at the earth below you and you look around at the scene of so much beauty where the stars seem to go on for ever. You then become very still within, there is a feeling of waiting and while you wait you make your intention to release the old and to embrace the new and to bring yourself back to life once again for we die and are reborn daily through our constant evolution into the light.

You become aware of something unravelling around you and you feel it unravel from your head to your toes and when all this unravelling has taken place you look and see that a cocoon has been removed from you and that cocoon transforms itself now into another shining star in the sky.

You feel a sense of freedom and you feel as though you are emerging, emerging from the old and into the new and as you connect to that feeling you are aware that you have huge butterfly wings which are beginning to open. As they unfold you realise that you are a butterfly and as the butterfly you can now fly across the universe and go where ever you wish. There is such a sense of freedom and playfulness within you for nothing is holding you back, you have your wings and you are free.

You realise that the old energies you were carrying were heavy even though you did not know it at the time but compared to the lighter vibration you have within you now there is no comparison.

You then fly down to the earth and you see before you many flowers in blossom and you fly from flower to flower drinking deeply of the sweet nectar and the feeling is of complete peace. You are free to play amongst the flowers and to go where you wish and you are free to drink from the sweetness of life for you have your wings and you can fly high.

The butterfly is an eternal symbol of the soul and with each unveiling and each uncovering of the old self we come closer to the revelation of the truth of who we are, of the light of divinity within us and the understanding that that light is connected to every other light within every other butterfly.

Fly high, leave the old behind and step into your freedom and the greatest freedom is just to be you.

Transformation

All your symptoms come from emotions you have held
in and where you have problems in your body it is
where the energy has condensed and become stuck.
To create healing you need to release and create a flow
once again but always remember that whatever you
release it is not sufficient just to release energy you
must look into it and feel all the emotions you have
never felt before and which you have pushed down.
You can do this healing either actually standing up or
just visualise that you are standing. Make your
intention to release all the stuck energies in your body
with your mind and then release them beginning at
your feet and working up to your crown. Where ever
you come to a place where you have a problem or pain
then release it upwards until you have released energy
from every part of you where you have discomfort.
Remember energy cannot be destroyed so you never
ever release without transforming what you release so
watch as all these stuck energies flow through your
crown and upwards and watch as all that energy
blends together and then creates the most brilliant star
then place that star in the heavens.

When we transform energies most of the time we transform and bring the transformed energy back into the body for more healing but occasionally we can release, transform and send out the energy in its purified state.

Look up into the heavens and see the bright star above you and feel all its radiant light shine down upon you.

Ascension Symptoms

There has been so much healing for everyone as we
have all delved deep within and we have had the time
to face ourselves more than ever before.

There has been much talk about ascension symptoms
and you may have learnt about this from other people
but the truth is there are no ascension symptoms there
are only your symptoms. What ever you are feeling
and whatever triggers you all that you feel within
comes from yourself. You cannot look to ascension
symptoms for making you feel as you do for they do
not exist. Yes we are moving into new times and our
consciousness is being raised constantly and yes we
are affected by outside forces and by the astrology of
the time but in the end everything comes back to you.
There are no ascension energies to make you feel as
you do for everything comes from within. Sometimes
the right conditions are provided for you by the
astrology of the time or by the behaviour of others but
these are just pointers showing you where to look
within. Claim everything as belonging to you and
when you have symptoms or when you are feeling

emotionally in pain then really connect in and see what is behind all these things.

Follow the trail to see what has caused these things within you even if it was another person who upset you, always dig deep within and find out what you are holding onto.

This is empowerment and this is what you have been working for to find your own power within you so that you do not give any of it away to anyone else and you claim it just for you. To be in your own power is such a great gift for you stand firm in your convictions and you judge no-one and eventually you do not even judge yourself.

If anyone tells you that what you are feeling are ascension symptoms then just know that they do not have the truth but maybe they are not ready to claim everything that they feel as belonging to them. We can pick up things from other people without a doubt but that is only because they reflect back to us what is already within us which needs healing.

So take the reins and be in your own light fully and your own power and do not let anyone take your light away ever again for it belongs to you and the truth is you gave it away in the first place but no more, this is your light and it shines so brightly when you see the truth of it of the divinity within.

In the same way as you cannot blame ascension symptoms on how you're feeling we often look outside of ourselves and ask all the saints and goddesses to heal us but the most powerful source of your own healing is the light within which is the divine within you, the spark of divinity, the unified force from where we all came.

So turn your prayers within in the light of the divine, the source of your light and connect to this and direct your attention to the greatest source of love, light and healing that you can ever find.

Take back your crown and know that all roads lead within.

Winter Solstice

Today is the winter solstice Eve and tomorrow we welcome back the sun as the light returns to us.
This winter solstice is a very important one as it marks a turning point, the astrology is very powerful at this time and it brings hope for us all. During the dark days of winter we connect to the depths within us and we go within and process those things which we still carry but today is the day to let them go so that tomorrow you can welcome back the sun.
This is the important time not Christmas Day for Christ was not even born then he was born on March 1st seven BC; the church took the old ways and made them their own. The world has stood still this year of the pandemic but now it turns once again as we move forward into the light.
Bringing in the sun is one of the most wonderful methods of healing and you can do this by visualising it at any time of day or night or any time of the year and it will bring immediate healing to you. The ancients knew the secrets of the sun and of sunlight and they used it for healing and awakening.

This solstice brings the golden fire, the golden fire of the new energies upon the earth and we can look upon this golden fire as the sun or actually as golden fire for they are one and the same and you can use it in any way you wish. Tomorrow go within and visualise the sun and feel its golden fire filling every part of you. Let it go to any pain or discomfort you have and watch that golden fire transform your aches and pains. Fill your aura with it so that you shine like the sun and become the sun yourself. Put the sun in your heart and see it radiate throughout the whole of your being bringing you peace in your heart and easing your pain. With the sun in your heart you become like a radio station receiving and giving out, receiving from spirit and then giving out the light to help others. When you work with the light in this way you are often not aware that you become a transmitting station shining your light onto others without you realising it and in this way we pass the light to each other.

Just know that this winter solstice is one of the most important ones you will ever have experienced so fill yourself to the brim with the sun so that we all become little suns shining the light in the darkness of the winter time. If you have been in your own internal winter dealing with sorrow and pain and loss and any other things then let yourself emerge now into the light for it is time to come out of the cave and to be in the light once again.

The goddess conceived a child at the spring equinox and at the winter solstice she gives birth to the golden child and a new cycle begins once again. Give birth to your own golden child from the sunlight within you and nurture it and love it and hold it close and watch as it grows further into the light.

These are important times more important than many realise and tomorrow the solar fire which has been building up in recent weeks will fill you completely if you allow it to. Shine bright with the fire and shine your light and your love for everyone to see.

The Rose Garden

This week our front garden has been completely transformed, all the old hedges have gone including the wall and new fencing has been erected around the boundaries so I have a new canvas now to create my rose garden. My roses are being delivered at the moment and I have other plants to plant out too. It is going to be a cottage garden filled with roses and my favourite cottage garden plants; it is not a huge space but it is more than enough for me.

This project feels so important to me and my Thursday evening zoom sessions at this time will now come from The Rose Garden. As I am creating a new rose garden on the physical level at the same time I am creating it on the etheric level in the realms of light. This is the same as Rose Cottage and the village of Rosmeade which are the subjects of my two Kindle books for eventually they took form in the light. The mind is the most powerful thing you have and we can create anything and it becomes real on another level. As we work towards the future of the new age of the Earth we will understand more and more how this works as we move into a time of manifestation through the mind.

My rose garden in the world of spirit is beginning to take form and it is vast not like an ordinary garden, it is not formal it has plants overflowing everywhere and it is packed with roses of every type. Even though this is just the beginning of this wonderful place in the realms of light I would like to invite you into it for healing and nurturing. I know how much some of you are struggling at this time for many reasons and I know how much you need healing and understanding and I also know how much you need the comfort and reassurance of nurturing energy so let me share this with you as I welcome you into my rose garden.

Sit quietly and go deep into your heart for the rose garden also resides within the heart. Feel yourself going deeper into it until eventually you can smell the perfume of roses.

You will find yourself standing at the entrance to an enormous garden and it is so huge that you cannot see the end of it and the perfume of it fills you completely and your whole being relaxes and lets go of all worldly worries. As you take your first step into the rose garden the Guardian of the garden comes forward and she looks like a beautiful fairy like being. Her clothes look as though they have been made from Rose petals and she has roses in her hair but more than anything it is her love which you feel directly come into your heart as she looks at you with so much love and she feels like a fairy godmother who has come to take care of you. As she shows you through the garden she points out all the beautiful things here. There are roses of every colour and there are marigolds and forget-me-nots, foxgloves, delphiniums and hollyhocks and so much more. It is like looking at a rainbow.

Eventually she will lead you to a round healing pool made of rose quartz crystal and filled with crystal clear water. The Guardian then tells you that this healing pool is filled with rose water and she asks you to step into the pool to receive all its blessings. As you lie within the water soaking up the glorious perfume you release all your worries and all your pain and all your stress into the water and as these things are released they transform into tiny pink roses. You find yourself then bathing not only in rose water but within a pool of roses and a great peace comes over you.

When your bathing is complete you step out of the water and the sun dries you completely and then the Guardian takes you to the most beautiful seat carved out of wood with roses carved within it and you sit together and face the West. As the sun sinks down to the horizon the sky takes on a rosy hue and your whole being is completely filled with the pink rays of the setting sun.

Deep Healing

We all have within us a core wound and it is this wound which we have brought into this life for our education and understanding and that wound motivates us until we can see the full truth of it and heal it. It is so important that you work with the things you have experienced in this life and it is only occasionally where you need to go back into another life to retrieve information.

I would like to share something with you about my own core wound. I always thought that it was guilt and indeed guilt has played a great part but I have discovered in recent years that it is actually loss and rejection and it has been a revelation to me. I know when it first began it was when I was six years old and it played a part without me realising it in a lot of situations in my life. I have no fear now of speaking out and if people choose to reject me it is no problem to me for that is healed within me but I am more aware now of instances where I could experience loss and rejection.

As you know and I have often talked about this I have lived with fear throughout my life and even though much of it is healed I'm still left with phobias and I am meant to be this way. My phobias centre around worrying about there being something wrong with my physical body but they are my greatest teachers showing me where to look to find wisdom. The body is the messenger and it carries great wisdom within it.

At one point I was worried about my heart, I knew it was all right but I explored it and a friend of mine who I trust told me this fear came from a previous life when I died from a heart problem after I gave birth. When I went into that life and re-experienced it I saw that the baby was my own mother and I realised that I have carried not only the guilt of leaving her but also a great sense of loss of having to leave my child behind when I passed over.

As I have reflected on so many experiences in my life I have discovered loss in everything and it has been a true revelation to me. Regarding that life I always thought it was the guilt that I carried from it but now I understand that loss is far more relevant and it puts a greater light on everything I have worked with for myself. My mother's core wound was loss and she passed that wound onto me along with fear and she taught me well.

Her wound began at three years old when her mother went to the shops and she stood gazing out of the window waiting for her to come back because she thought she had abandoned her. Her father told her to stop crying and so the energy of it would have been held within so everything for her went back to that. Throughout her life even until she was an old lady when I visited her if I went out to do shopping or to visit someone if I was a minute late she would stand at the door or the window thinking that I wouldn't be coming back.

We even have a funny story about this when my brother visited her and he went out with his friends for the night and he was around the age of 40, she called the police thinking he wasn't coming back so you can understand how deep this went within.

What I find most interesting is that I am named after my mother's mother and apparently I am very like her so my mother feared the loss of her mother whom she thought had abandoned her and then in my previous life with her I abandoned her too by dying. I have received now a much deeper understanding of the thing which has driven my life and I am so very grateful for this. My teachings come from my life's experiences for life is the greatest teacher of all and you too have your teachings from what you have experienced.

Your body is your teacher telling you where to look by understanding the symbolism and the messages which the body brings. By becoming like a detective and exploring these hidden messages you will discover what emotions lie behind any of your problems and then the healing can begin.

Life is an adventure and we come here to school to learn so that we are free of those things we have carried from lifetime to lifetime then we can share them with others as I share them with you so that I can help you to find out what is at the very bottom of all the things which cause you pain and distress. Become an explorer and find your answers and find your core wound and love it for all the blessings and teachings it has brought to you.

The Mary Flame

Here is the new healing flame brought to you from
Mary Magdalene and it is called the Mary Flame. It is a
pink rose flame but it is actually made of roses and the
centre is golden fire like the gold which you will find
at the very centre of a rose.

The roses of this flame are the roses called Maria. This
is not like any other rose flame you will have heard of
for it is actually made of roses and when you stand
within it you will be able to smell the perfume of the
roses and you will feel the softness of the petals.

Like all healing flames this is actually a flame shape
and the roses which it is made of are made of fire and
the very centre of the rose is the gold which you will
always find there and the centre of this flame is the
golden fire.

This flame comes from Mary Magdalene and it is
brought to you for you to delve so deep within to bring
yourself the most profound healing you have ever had.
If you are tired of working with the same emotions
again and again step into this flame, see your whole
self stepping within it and let it bring to the surface the
remnants of anything which now is ready to be

released. The key to all this as with all healing is to feel completely every emotion which comes up and feel it like never before.

As you do this the gold at the centre of this flame will bring you the wisdom and understanding while the pink roses of the outer flame will bring you great love, compassion and self forgiveness.

This sacred flame is brought to you from the rose Maria and from Mary Magdalene and it is brought with the greatest love for you.

Healing The Roots

Yesterday when I got up I found a pink geranium flower outside the front door and it had blown over from one of my pots and I knew that this was the colour of the day and the colour which I needed to take in. Just after that I had a delivery of a rose which I have been waiting for and it is a pink rose the same colour as my geranium and it is called Maria.

I had searched for a rose called Mary to celebrate Mary Magdalene and I could not find one apart from one called Mary Rose and I didn't want a rose named after a ship which had sunk. There was an actual rose called Mary Magdalene but it is no longer for sale. I was delighted to receive this rose and I knew that it was right on time for yesterday Mary Magdalene had information to share with me. She brings you now a message but she also brings to you a new healing flame which I have shared with you.

All your healing leads back to the root cause, to the time when the first emotional patterns were planted within you and from then these patterns grew and blossomed and caused you much pain as they attracted the same lessons to you over and over again. To heal yourself you heal your roots and these roots can be traced back to when the original pain was felt by you but the time comes when the pain which was repressed and left deep within you is ready to rise up to the surface to be looked at and transformed and healed. This time is so important for the healing of your roots and if you would take the time to go deep within back to the beginning and find the root cause of any of your emotional pain you will find that you have access to great healing and understanding so that those patterns which you have carried with you throughout your life can be disarmed and you can begin again with a set of new patterns.

Healing comes on many levels and you often return time and time again to the same things which have caused you distress and each time you go a little deeper and each time you receive more understanding but now those roots within you are ripe and ready to be discovered. Once you discover the one main root you can dig it up and look at it with new eyes and to do that you need to feel all your pain every last drop of it and when you have emptied out you can look at the root and look at all the people involved within that root and you will see that they too had deep roots of pain within them as well.

You will also see that they were your teachers for without them you would not have been able to learn the life's lessons which you returned to experience. You came into this life with a mission and that was to heal those things which you have carried within you from lifetime to lifetime and you do not need to go back into the past of other lives all you need to do is to go back into the past of this lifetime and find when your emotional patterns were conceived.

To heal yourself in this way is total liberation for it sets you free to be who you truly are instead of being motivated by your conditioning, this is the true freedom. By healing yourself in this way you are also given the skills to heal others in the same way.

Go to your roots for it is time, the energies are just right for this delving deep and the alignments in the heavens are right also to bring you the sacred space to dive deep. I have brought to you a new flame to help you with this healing and I gave it a name of the Mary flame. My work is to help you to heal by bringing you not only love and truth but also self forgiveness for there is no one else to forgive only yourself for you never did anything wrong you only did the best you could. So find it all and feel it all then love yourself more fiercely than you ever have done before and that love and letting go will bring you the greatest healing of all.

The Rose

The rose has long been associated with the spiritual self, it is an ancient flower with ancient roots and for many reasons it has been a symbol of spirituality. We know it more than anything at this time as the symbol of Mary Magdalene but it has also been associated with Mary the mother and many other saints but it is Magdalene's rose which is more relevant now than any other.

The rose carries much symbolism within it, even the name, rose, is what we are all doing as we rise up and journey into ascension. The rose itself is the story of our lives as we travel from the roots and deal with the thorny situations of our lives until we blossom and bloom with the greatest beauty from all the wisdom we acquire.

The pentagram is underneath the rose in its five sepals and it carries the five pointed star within it, the mark of the goddess, the star of Venus and the map of the five elements, the foundation of much healing medicine. The rose itself carries very powerful healing properties within it and so we can understand why it is called the queen of flowers.

The stained glass rose in the window of the original front door in our bungalow is made in the style of Rennie Mackintosh and I was drawn to it yet again yesterday. As I looked at its colours in the leaded window it was the gold at the very centre of it which drew my attention and it is the gold at the very centre of any rose which means the most to us.

The most important message of Mary Magdalene is that everything is within; god goddess is within, everything you need to know is within and even though we search without for answers all the answers and all the wisdom is within us already.

Our inner world is rich with wisdom and many realms of light for you have everything within you, you have worlds within worlds, whole universes within you.

You can enter within and explore all the kingdoms of nature and all the kingdoms of the heavens as well for it is all within.

One of the ways to access your inner world is through the heart and the rose is the heart and it is the soul as well so to work with the rose is to enter the heart space and the soul.

The rose has been part of the teachings of many now in recent years for it is always part of the divine feminine wisdom which is now more apparent than ever before but there is so much to the rose which is still to be revealed to us. You can use the rose to enter within to reach those parts of you which will bring you wisdom, solace and healing.

Place a multicoloured rose within your heart and then enter into the very centre of the rose within your heart, enter into the golden fire in the very middle of the rose and immerse yourself in this golden fire and feel the multicoloured petals of the rose softly holding you.

As you enter into this golden fire you will eventually see before you a golden door and when you walk through that door you will enter into another realm, another world and each time you enter it it will be different. You may enter a meadow on a sunny summer's day and you can go and sit amongst the wildflowers and communicate with the insects or you may find yourself high up in the mountains where you can meet the sages from time gone by.

Through this door you can enter the starry heavens and travel across the universe and meet with the light beings who are the guardians of our planet or you may just find yourself in a cosy room sitting by the fire. Remember your inner world is rich beyond your wildest dreams so journey there often and use the rose as your gateway and remember the rose is your soul and your soul is part of the divine and not separate from anything at all.

The Gift

Last week I took a different route on my walk to the beach and it was one I haven't been along for a little while. I was amazed by so many gardens still having lots of flowers in them but there was one particular one I passed which was absolutely stunning. It was jam packed with flowers and it was so beautiful. I stopped to stare at it and take everything in. There were lots of chrysanthemums in bloom, these are not flowers I have been fond of but they looked so lovely I thought I must now try and grow them.

Yesterday I decided to take my usual route to the beach but something told me to take the other way so that I could go and look at that garden again. As I approached the house there was a couple outside and so I thought I had better just walk slowly so that I could enjoy it without appearing too nosey. The lady there came over to me and she began to talk to me. I told her how beautiful I thought that the garden was, it was spilling over with different flowers and the borders were full to the brim with marigolds one of my favourite flowers.

She asked me if I would like some of her flowers and I said it was enough for me just to admire them but she insisted and picked a bunch of yellow chrysanthemums for me and I thought it was so kind of her. As we chatted and shared our love of flowers she went over to the other side of the garden and picked me a bunch of pink and white chrysanthemums as well. She was so kind and I was deeply touched by her generosity.

I decided to retrace my steps and go back home and I felt like the child again for when I was little I never returned home without flowers in my hands and there was always a bunch for my mammy and a bunch for my teacher. To this day I always take flowers when I visit someone.

As I reflected upon this event and I saw the magic in it I also saw that the flowers I had been gifted were ones that I had not previously been fond of. These were flowers which only the week before I thought I might start to grow and I was in awe that such magic can happen when you least expect it. The lady even explained to me how to propagate plants from the flowers she had given me so that I can grow on my own chrysanthemums from her gift.

I love the magic of life and it is much needed by everyone and it is the magic and the little things and

the magic in the kindness which means so much.
Chrysanthemums happen to be the flowers which
represent mums and when you receive them very often
your own mum is around you or the mother energy so
I knew that I had been deeply blessed by so much in
many more ways than I could imagine

The Altar

Graham and I decided to buy some storage cupboards for the room we both work in and they arrived last week. I had a bookshelf in here which also doubled up as my altar and it had been there for many years and for all the years where I held spiritual groups here. I decided it was time for the bookshelf to go and so my new altar would be the tops of both cupboards.

So I emptied everything from my altar and placed just some of the things back again on top of each cupboard and now I have two altars. I don't like a lot of things around me, I'm quite minimalist, I am the opposite in the garden where I will squeeze as many flowers in as I can but inside I like space around me. So I set up my new altars and reflected upon this because everything we do around us reflects back to us what is going on within, the whole world is just one huge mirror.

The altar is the self and what ever you put upon it is what you are surrounding yourself with so that when you make changes and bring new things in you are also bringing new energies in for yourself and you are altering certain things. The altar is about altering. Traditionally an altar is changed according to each sabbat with each turn of the wheel of the year but I don't like to follow rules regarding spiritual matters I prefer to follow what I feel personally.

Usually people will put things upon their altars to reflect the changing seasons and the eight festivals of the year and I teach this to my priestesses so that they can see in front of them the changing energies. If you haven't got an altar then it is a wonderful thing to have, you can dedicate a table to it or use your hearth or even use the top of a bookcase like I did or a cupboard or you can have an outside altar. You can then see it as a reflection of you of where you are at this very moment then when you are urged to make changes upon it you will know that this is showing you that you are ready for changes yourself.

You can put things upon it to represent the four elements, incense for air, candles for fire, flowers for earth and water for the water element. You can bring in a chalice and if you do not have one you can use a nice glass; the chalice represents the divine feminine and it is a reminder of this. You can then place what ever you wish upon the altar, pictures, statues, crystals and see it as a mirror of you.

Connecting to an altar brings you the outward manifestation of what is within you for connecting to the altar is about connecting deep within yourself and to the divine light which runs through all things. So enjoy your sacred space of your altar and remember always it needs continual change.

The Violet

I have just received a vision which I would like to share with you. It came in first of all as an incredible green mist. Just after that I found some soil on the kitchen floor and I don't know where it came from and I held it in my hands and felt the brown earth. Immediately I sat outside and felt all the green around me and the mist changed into the most amazing scene for I was taken way back in time before humans emerged.

I was shown the luscious scenery where everything was so green, there were huge waterfalls and abundant forests. There were birds of the brightest colours and exotic flowers. This was the earth when just the animals roamed it before humanity came to be. It was pristine and extremely beautiful and yet at the same time it felt to me that it was not a safe place for there were so many wild animals everywhere.

It was an amazing experience and as I reflected upon it I was shown that many do not feel safe today in our present world for different reasons, they feel threatened by people and by everything which is going on and yet all that is happening in the outer world is change and this reflects our inner worlds where we are changing alongside this.

I was then shown many violets and these flowers are so very special and very sacred, they are the flowers of the heart but they also carry within them the violet ray and within the violet ray nothing negative can exist. This is why many people use the violet flame for healing. The colour of violet is the colour of magic and transformation and magic is transformation and transformation is change.

For all that we are experiencing in the world today it is only change that is all it is and we are in the midst of that change and the purple violet which came in today is to show you that this is where we are all at and it is where mother earth is at as well for we are going through times of transformation and nothing can change within or without without there being adjustments.

From the violet I then saw the purple heart, the badge of honour for people who have been through a war and I would like to share the purple heart but the war we are fighting is not with the virus or with all that goes on in the world it is the transformation within where we battle to face the truth of ourselves and then to show that truth to the world. So wear your purple heart with pride for you are part of the change and just as the world I was shown so long ago was ready to change with the evolution of humanity we are going through another evolution now as we evolve into beings of light while being fully present here upon the earth.

The Candle

Recently I was talking to my sister and she told me that she still has a candle which I brought back from Switzerland for her 50 years ago and she has taken it with her each time she moved house. It brought back all the memories of that holiday and it was something I had forgotten all about.

I was at college at the time and along with two other girls we hitchhiked down the Rhine in Germany and then throughout Switzerland and we had the most amazing time. It was safer in those days to hitchhike. I remembered about the candles and how I had bought lots of them in Switzerland and they were covered in Edelweiss and alpine flowers and I bought one each for my parents, my sister, my brother, my aunties and some friends as well and I carried them in my rucksack, goodness knows how I did it.

As I reflected upon it I saw the candles as the light for the candle always symbolises bringing in the light and my sister has had that light with her all these years. We give our light out to each other without realising it, we give our light out in many ways and that light touches people and so we become the candle and then we light the candles of others. They then go on to further light other people's candles so we pass the light around. Sometimes our light burns low and at other times it is a great big flame and there are those times where our light goes out and it needs to be reignited again, reignited with wisdom and love. Our light shines bright just like the flame of the candle and although we cannot see the flames of others they are there and we recognise the light of another person often without any words, it is something we just know.

If you feel that your own light burns low then visualise yourself as the candle and with your mind expand your flame so that it shines so brightly and you too will feel much brighter. Each day shine your light and expand your light and if you are feeling low then turn up that light.

Sometimes when we have a lot of light it shines the light on things we do not like to face, things we do not like to see but it is only by putting everything into the light that we can get to the truth of all things. We are attracted by each other's light that is why people are drawn to you and they feel the warmth from that light and that warmth warms them on the days when life is cold.

Shine bright and you will feel what a difference it can make when you become the flame upon your candle for the candle is the physical self and the flame is your spiritual self and the two are as one. When you light your candles in your home just look and see how they are a reflection of you and when you look into the magnificent golden flame you will understand that that light is within you also. Shine bright for yourself and for everyone else around you.

The Lime Tree

I know all the trees which grow along the river where I walk and there is one which I have a great affinity for and it is a linden or lime tree which I greatly love. It stands next to a smaller tree the same as itself but I have only ever gone to connect to one of them. I was never drawn to the other one or to its energy. The one I connect to is a beautiful tree with a great canopy of branches to stand beneath. I love this tree and I hug it and communicate with it and I wait every year for its beautiful flowers which have the most amazing perfume. Strangely enough the second tree never seems to have many flowers.

Yesterday when I went to the tree I usually go to I was told to go and connect to the one next to it which I did but when I put my arms around it there was the most incredible feeling of sadness. It communicated to me that it had watched me for over 20 years loving the other tree and yet I had never given this one any love at all. I felt this most profoundly so I loved that tree for the first time.

As I was connecting to it I was shown the meaning of this for nature has much to teach us and much to share with us. I had always seen the tree I connected to as feminine and the one I stayed away from as masculine. I then understood what this meant.

During these times where we are reclaiming the divine feminine aspect of ourselves we sometimes forget that we need the divine masculine as well for we have to have balance. The feminine energy is rising in the world out of oppression and suppression and there is still much work to be done but this does not imply that the female energy will be any greater than the male energy, this is about restoring balance.

I often find that with many of the women I work with who have been repressed it is not their feminine side which needs healing it is their male side, the divine male within. It is the male aspect of us whether we are male or female which is free to speak out and be assertive. I had shied away from my masculine side for a good part of my life never allowing myself to be truly assertive and so I denied part of me.

I have learnt now to be assertive and I will never go back to the person I was before for it is too painful to live like that but what I realised as I connected to the linden trees was that at the time when I first had a dislike of the male tree it was because I was frightened of that side of me, I was frightened to own it. So I was still living in the past when I looked at that linden tree because now I embrace both the divine feminine and the divine masculine.

In that moment of realisation I loved the tree some more and I saw for all those years why I was reluctant to go near it, it was only an old energy.

It is interesting that the linden tree is the tree of the heart for its leaves are heart shaped, it is such an incredibly healing tree and it brought me the most wonderful lesson one which I already understood but one which I needed to hear again and that is that we need to have the complete balance of both male and female energies within us. At the same time the future of the Earth is never about division it is about oneness, equality, balance and harmony so that the divine feminine and the divine male will be at one within each of us.

Joseph Of Arimathea

Joseph of Arimathea has always been quoted as being the uncle of Jesus but he was the brother of Jesus and his true name was James. The names Joseph and Arimathea were titles bestowed upon people and this was the case with many names in the Bible, the names were descriptive of who they were or their profession. Joseph was a trader of metals and he traded with Britain in the West Country and on one occasion he brought one of the children of Jesus and Mary Magdalene with him and this child was also called Jesus. It is thought that Jesus himself came to Britain but he didn't it was his son Jesus who came with his uncle, Joseph of Arimathea and so it was the son of Jesus who walked this land.

There are many who think Mary Magdalene came to Britain as well but I have never believed this but again all these things are my personal beliefs and we all have our own truth.

Joseph was given land in Glastonbury and he built the first church there and dedicated it to Mary Magdalene for it was built in the year of her death. The little church was in what are now the grounds of Glastonbury Abbey.

The bloodline of Jesus and Mary Magdalene as was that of Joseph of Arimathea the brother of Jesus has come through its lineage in Britain, through King Arthur and many other famous people and so the lineage of Jesus and Mary Magdalene runs through British soil and no doubt although we are a mix of many races in Britain that lineage will have followed through.

Always question what you read including what I write and there are many who channel books about Mary Magdalene and Jesus, question those as well and in the end let your own heart tell you what is the truth for you.

Aquamarine

Yesterday a huge blue bird came to me and told me it was the spirit of healing and each time it flapped its wings it sent healing vibrations out to whoever needed it. Blue is the colour of healing and it is also the colour of the water element.

All shades of blue bring healing but at this very moment the blue which can heal you is aquamarine or turquoise blue for this is the colour of the new and it is the colour which will lead you out of the old and into the new. There are so many ways to heal but eventually there will be only one way and that is through pure wisdom for it is the wisdom which comes from the self, the divine self within which will always show you the way, the divinity within which has all the answers.

The world is shifting from the old to the new and when this current virus has run its course as viruses do the world will be different and the world needs to change and we too need to change. If you want to heal then bring the blue around you and bring the aquamarine colours of the new world and sit within that light or delve deep into the ocean.

Then ask yourself if you are living the life you want to live or are you just half living and compromising. If the answer is that you are not living in your full power doing what you want to do without any one person not honouring you then bring in the changes and begin today. All you need to do is to make the decision that you want a better life and a happier life and a more fulfilling life.

You can go to as many healers as you wish and receive so many wonderful healings but until you change within your life will not change. The change comes from when you access the newness of thinking with the belief that you can create the life you want and the peace you want and then you take action. Taking action often means honouring what you believe then speaking your truth to others and letting them know what you do and do not want.

Why stay in a job which does not feed you and why stay in a relationship which does not respect you? The answer to this is fear, the fear of change and we have all been there, I have been there and it is all about fear. People make excuses for why they remain in situations which have served their purpose and they know within they are scared of the unknown and that is understandable.

We are all linked and we are linked with the world around us and what we do as individuals affects the collective and when we make a change then the world changes too. This is the butterfly effect for when one butterfly flaps its wings the whole universe feels it and is changed. Are you claiming your wings, do you fly high, have you got the freedom to do what you want to do? If you haven't then make a start today

The old energy is tired and you feel it and you become tired because it is heavy and you carry it within you never feeling fully on fire and fully alive. You hold in what you believe and what you feel for the fear of how others may respond to you but you deserve so much better. Step into the new energy, step into the aquamarine, step into the turquoise waters and connect to the water which holds all the memories of this planet and feel the expansion which this brings to you.

This new light waits for you for you to be fully immersed within it, the aquamarine or turquoise energy is the ancient wisdom brought in to modern times and it is the colour of our future world.

Give yourself permission to embrace the aquamarine and let it fill you every day and it will make you stronger and it will disarm your fear so that you take the reins and become in charge of your own life then you will feel empowered in a way you never have before. This is love; this is the greatest love when you hear the call of the divinity within to journey home to your true self who is radiant with light and truth.

Energies

Often the people I teach will ask me questions about the spiritual path and I will provide the answers but sometimes I feel that the questions they ask are very important and so I would like to share a recent question which someone asked me with you all.

The subject was about entities and attachments. Here I will give my own beliefs on these, please remember that we are all individual and we see things in different ways, these are my thoughts.

Entities and attachments which people see are not that, they are manifestations of the thought forms of the person before you. Many famous teachers still teach about entities and attachments and dark entities and this creates much fear and people believe them. Our thoughts create our reality; thoughts are the most powerful things.

What people see as a dark entity attached to a person is the energy from the person's thoughts in the person you are connecting to. These thoughts have manifested as what we would call negative energy around them. The truth is there is no negative energy there is only energy but we can call it negative because it is stuck and condensed and old.

I don't doubt that people see these and sense them but the truth is they are only picking up and seeing what is projected from that person. Sometimes if a person is very depressed they may feel they have a spirit entity attached to them but this is not so it is because they have gone on to a very low vibration within themselves and their thoughts have condensed around them and their energies feel very dark and uncomfortable.

There is so much said now in videos and in posts about removing entities, attachments and all manner of things and I often write about this but I write about it because it is a subject which comes up time and time again. People teach others how to remove all these things but the truth is they do not have the true understanding about energy.

It is the same with ghosts, ghosts are energies which have been left behind in a place and they can be seen as real as any person. Kryon channelled by Lee Carroll describes it beautifully when he says it is like leaving a stain behind.

We are the creators of our own universe and our own reality and when our thoughts become stagnant and stuck they gather around us like old grey cotton wool and they feel heavy and they make us tired but it is only old energy.

If someone tells you that they feel ill after working with a person and that they have picked all sorts up from them it is because there is something within them which needs to be healed and it mirrors the energy of the person they are working with. We always have to come back to the self and this is a universal truth and as time goes on this will be the basis of all spiritual teachings as we learn to manifest with the mind. Please do not listen to anyone who is peddling fear and teaching you to detach entities from other people or to take out implants or who is telling you to protect yourself, their teachings belong in the past and they are not relevant now. The energies around us belong to us, we created them with our minds and if we do pick things up from other people it is because we need to feel their pain so that we can help them through understanding their pain or it is because we have the same thing inside us. Remember like attracts like, as you think so you become and what you give out comes back to you. This was the wonderful saying of the great healer Louise Hay.

If you are tired or if you feel out of sorts or if someone has upset you or you have not been well then your energy may need changing so instead of looking to an outside cause or to ascension energies or to what someone else has done instead use the magic of transformation. Feel what is around you, see what it is, see the truth of it and then transmute it into healing light and put it back within your energy field.

Every thought has incredible power and this is why the future will be golden and way ahead in years to come we will harness the power of the mind to create only good as we spread love through our manifestations for the good of all.

Transforming Energies

When you feel tired or not your best the key to changing energies is always transformation and what this means is that you never ever discard stagnant old energy, you never throw it away and you never put it in the earth you always change it and transmute it into something else. However first of all you feel what is in that energy and you do this whether you are working with it for yourself or for someone whom you are healing, you always feel the emotions within the energy so that you can understand what has caused the person to feel as they do.

If you are feeling tired, if you have something on your mind, if someone has caused you pain, if you find you cannot let go of your thoughts or if you are not feeling well or even if you have had an argument with someone the energy will often gather around you and it can feel very heavy.

You can change your energy immediately and it does not have to take time it can take just a few seconds and you will feel the difference straightaway so here are some suggestions for you to try and maybe to share with people whom you help.

Visualise that you are a tree covered with old dead leaves and those leaves are your old thoughts and old energies; call upon the wind and ask the wind to come and blow them all from you so that you are left with bare branches. Watch as the leaves fall from you into a pile and with your mind you are to visualise it lit. All the old leaves will then burn away and they will leave in their place a diamond and you take that diamond and place it in your heart; the Diamond light then spreads through every part of you.

You can visualise yourself as a diamond and feel yourself rising up into the blue sky where the sun shines brightly through every facet of your diamond and it burns away any old energy you are carrying and transforms it all into rainbows of light. This is a wonderful healing to do.

I find that the sun is one of the greatest transformers of all and so if you visualise the sun shining upon you just where you are and let it fill you with its golden light it will transform all the old energy within you and it will create an even greater light so that you feel energised and uplifted.

See yourself standing on the top of a mountain and call the wind and feel the wind blow away all the cobwebs around you. Cobwebs are very healing but they represent old energy; as the cobwebs flow from you they gather up together so visualise them transforming into a beautiful iridescent coat and you put that coat on.

When the energy in your aura feels tired and heavy it can feel like an old coat so visualise yourself taking it off and look and see what feelings are within it and then transform it into a brand-new coat made of brilliant light and put it back on.

Visualise yourself in a river and feel the water flowing through you. Old energy is just stagnant energy and when you feel tired your energy is not flowing properly. As the water flows through you it flushes out the old energies from you to the water but remember you must never leave stagnant energy lying around or someone else will pick it up so as this old energy leaves your body visualise it turning into beautiful water lilies.

Old energy belongs to us for we have created it within our minds but we can transform energies and use them for the earth but the earth does not transform energies for you so never put anything in it which has not been turned back to the light.

Visualise starlight entering your crown and moving down through the whole of your body and out through the soles of your feet where it pushes out your old energies. Change the old energy which you have released into beautiful white light and send that energy into the earth for the good of all. Although we can do this to help the earth the majority of times you need to take that energy back to yourself because it belongs to you.

There are so many ways of changing your energy all it takes is your imagination so you release, you feel and you transform and you receive the transformed energy back into your energy field.

Using any of these techniques or any that you can create yourself will always make you feel better straightaway. Your thoughts create the energy around you and your thoughts can also change the energy. I do not believe in protection because that is based upon fear but I do believe that we need to do a housecleaning on our own energies whenever we feel the need. However it is important not to become obsessive about this, just do it when you feel you need to be energised and renewed.

Enjoy your transformations and see how many you can create for yourself and each day you will live even more in the light but it is the light which brings understanding and it is the understanding of what you are carrying in your energy field which will bring you great healing.

Healing

This was given to me so I will share it with you and it will bring you the most wonderful feeling of healing and support today.

Call in a brilliant white light; surround yourself with it and let that light lift you up higher and higher. Eventually you will feel yourself surrounded everywhere with even more white light and from that light will emerge white butterflies. The butterfly is a symbol of the soul.

You will feel as though you are surrounded by many beings of light and the feeling of support will be overwhelming and you will know without a doubt that you are held and supported and loved by many unseen beings.

As you watch the butterflies encircling you and fluttering their wings they will each begin to take on a very pale shade of a colour.

They will continue to do this until you are surrounded by many colourful butterflies but there will be one which will stand out and it will come to you.

It will surround you and flutter its wings and as it moves around you it will totally transform your energy.

You are then to come back into your body but the butterfly with its beautiful colour will still be there fluttering around you and after a little while it will manifest as a spiritual guide for you.

This is the one who is with you holding your hand supporting you and looking after you so let them take care of you. Share anything with them which may concern you and allow yourself to be held in the love from your beautiful helper.

Hugs

I was very fortunate to have been brought up in a wonderful family with very loving parents but in those days people did not really hug one another like they do now and so I was not really used when I was young to hugging friends. Then when I began to explore the spiritual path and I attended meetings it was so lovely and so friendly and everyone hugged one another. When the time came for me to run my own workshops and classes no-one escaped a hug. There were hugs at the beginning and everyone hugged one another at the end. There was always so much love and warmth between us all. I remember once hugging someone and they told me I was doing it the wrong way. I am left-handed and I always hug to the left but he told me that the right way was to do it to the right so that your heart would touch the heart of the person you were hugging but to me it doesn't matter for a hug is a hug and it is certainly a meeting heart to heart whichever side you go to.

During the strange times of covid many people have been deprived of hugs and if you live on your own you must miss immensely the close contact of someone else. Even when we meet our friends now we have to keep our distance so there are many who have had no physical contact for a long time. If you live with someone else then you have many opportunities to enjoy hugging but for those of you who live alone it must be hard. People have sent virtual hugs around and that is very nice but I want to offer to you today a hug from me, not a virtual one but a hug done soul to soul.

I invite you to come to my garden, the place you will always find me and we will hug and our hearts will connect and you will feel the warmth which comes from human physical contact. No matter how spiritual you might be you need the physical presence and physical touch of another person. At this time and for the foreseeable future you are being denied this and it must seem a long time since some of you felt the closeness of others or that closeness of your close friends when you meet.

We are spiritual beings living in a physical body and it is so important that we are fully present and grounded and rooted in mother Earth. There are many meditations we can do with our wonderful spiritual teachers and we can bask in their light and their loving presence but nothing will ever replace a human hug.

So I invite you to my garden to meet me and I will wrap my arms around you and hold you close and our hearts will beat together and I will tell you that everything will be all right.

Fear

I often speak about fear because fear is something I brought with me into this life, it has always been part of me and it always will be. I am meant to be this way so that I can teach others about fear and so that they understand and accept it. Most of my fears have been healed through understanding but I still have some left within me and it makes me who I am. People sometimes think that to do spiritual work you have to be healed of everything but this is not the case for we are human and our healing never stops.

I share these things with you so that you can look to your own fears and anxieties and know that it is all right to have them and for you not to feel any shame with them. I have had many fears from big ones to little ones and bit by bit I worked through many of them and also I saw the humour in them for they were so funny at times. My biggest fear is being fearful of any symptoms in my body, they have terrified me and I mean real terror for the fear of what might happen to me. The body is the teacher so I learnt that each symptom is just a message from my soul to show me what emotions I am holding in.

I remember once a long time ago I woke in the middle of the night and the veins were standing out on my feet and I was terrified. The next day I walked to my friend's house and I told her all about it as between us we often discussed fear as she was the same as me. How blessed I was to have a friend who suffered as I did. When I arrived at her house she turned to her husband and said, "Do you know that Peg has walked all the way down here and she described all sorts of terrible illnesses to do with the circulation". We then just laughed and laughed for humour disarms fear.

I speak of these things not for sympathy for that is something I would never ever want I speak about them to reveal to you what I have within me so that you can also reveal what you have inside you without any feelings of shame.

One of the biggest fears I developed was of people putting things upon me that I didn't want to do and this was big because at that time I had no voice and I couldn't speak my truth. I drew into my life many people who were controlling but we can never blame anyone else we always have to bring everything back to ourselves for I was responsible for not speaking out. That fear has long gone for I would not hesitate for a second to speak out and answer back now and I will allow no-one to be disrespectful to me but it took a long time to get to that place and it took a lot of practice.

I had a recurring dream from when I was about 14 until I was about 50 where I was being chased, I was always running away from someone and it is quite funny but it was often the Nazis. This does not relate to a past life at all it is just symbolic. I would wake up screaming and shouting and terrified. As time went on I began to understand what it was about as I also began to speak out. It always happened when someone was trying to make me do something I did not want to do. I often did what others wanted as I was always a people pleaser and I did not have no in my vocabulary. What I was doing was pushing down my true feelings squashing them until so much piled up within me and each time something happened I would run away from what I was feeling and push it down even more. My goodness I was full to the brim. The subconscious finds a way out to the surface during dreamtime for our dreams are symbolic, they are not past lives they are fully about the present. So for many years I dreamt I was being chased in the most horrific way but the truth was I was running away from owning my feelings and speaking out.

When I look back and see the damage I have done to myself through countless years of pleasing other people and not saying what I really felt it is huge. It all comes down not only to the fear of speaking out but it is about the fear of rejection and that always comes back to lack of self-love. Now I don't mind who I speak my truth to and those who do not like it then that is their problem not mine however in the past I couldn't cope with the feelings of guilt and rejection so I went along with so much controlling behaviour.

Having said all this, what a wonderful education I have had and what wonderful teachers I have had also who had come to control me and make me do what they wanted and they have rejected me when I didn't do as they wished. No book could have taught me this. I have been truly blessed with all my fears; I brought them with me from lifetime to lifetime. People will often say well you can heal all these things but the truth is no you can't always because they are our teachers and we have come here to school to learn to receive the teachings of life and then to help others in their journeys.

I have written a lot about truth and about speaking out for many of the people I teach come with fear for they too have been controlled and squashed but I can honestly say to them I understand.

There is a great beauty in these teachings and the teachings of fear and I know fear and I know the fear

which brings so much terror you just want to run away but fear has and still continues to be my best friend for it has taught me so very much. I no longer scream in the night or dream that I am being chased and I no longer allow anyone to put anything upon me and I no longer say yes when I mean no but I am still learning as we all are, learning and healing some more.
So when you come to me and tell me about your fears and what has happened to you and how hard you find it to speak out to others to give them your truth I can truthfully say I do understand.

Lunch Date

Graham and I haven't had many date nights this year so I suggested we had a date lunch today and we went down to the beach here where we live where there is a hut selling chips and all sorts of other things. The tables and chairs outside had all been removed because of covid restrictions but it was still as busy as it always is.

We enjoyed our lunch of mushy pea fritters and chips, a perfect meal for two vegans and we appreciated so much such a simple pleasure. It was sunny and warm and the tide was right out with the Irish Sea in front of us and a view of Liverpool to one side with the Welsh mountains on the other side with Moel Famau as always rising above it surroundings.

We haven't been able to go out this year as we normally would and we haven't been able to meet our friends and share nice dinners together but in spite of that there has been so much to be appreciative of.

The little green hut at the beach was as good as any fine dining and I have met friends there during these recent times and enjoyed a walk with them. I know that all of you reading this will appreciate all that you have during this year and we have learned to appreciate things just that bit more and it is the simplest things which mean more than anything else. We appreciate our friends and our family more than ever and the simple pleasures like mushy pea fritters and chips at the beach can never compare at this time with more exotic locations. So Graham and I enjoyed our date lunch with much appreciation. There were many other people there enjoying their outing the same as we were and as the world turns inward once again we count our blessings in the simplest of things.

Mushy Peas

I share stories with you so that if anything within them touches something within you you can know that you are not on your own with what you have experienced. During the week a friend who I trust sent me a text message and she described how she saw me and I was in my early 20s and she said I was to go back and reclaim something I had left behind. With her description of what she saw I knew immediately what she was referring to and it was when I was 21 when someone tried to rape me. I have written about this before and I remember then many people responded that similar things had happened to them but I feel the need to write about it again because of what I discovered.

This is healed within me and I never look for any sympathy and I don't want sympathy for any of my experiences but there is more to the story than I originally thought. It happened during the night when I first began teaching and I shared a house with four other people. Afterwards we called in the police and the man was eventually found and prosecuted but I went to school as normal that day after they had been.

This shows how much I repressed my emotions. My partner at the time who I subsequently married and later divorced could not handle what had happened and so we never spoke about it and I never spoke about it afterwards either to anyone.

It was only when years later I stepped onto the path of self-healing that I dealt with this and healed it. I had not thought about it for a while but after my friend shared her message with me I went out into the garden and revisited that time. I had just had my 21st birthday and I smoked then and someone had given me a gold cigarette lighter which he stole, this is symbolic of him stealing my light so when I went back I saw that he had taken my light and I brought the light back with me. We give away our light but some people take our light as well.

He held a knife at my throat and I saw once again how much it had damaged my throat chakra; I was a quiet person anyway and I held in my feelings and did not speak out but on looking back I saw how much my ability to speak out deteriorated from that time. So what I saw and what I reclaimed was the light of greater understanding on how my throat chakra had been so blocked. It is certainly not blocked now I won't put up with a single thing and I will always speak out and I am still learning.

As I reflected I was taken forward in time to when there was a very powerful female in my life who was always trying to make me do things I didn't want to do and at that time I had not reclaimed my voice. The strangest thing was that when she particularly tried to put things on me I would always have sexual dreams about a man I had known in my past but I never fully understood why these dreams came and what they were really trying to tell me. I just interpreted them as her trying to enter my personal space but there was one particular time and the last time she did it where she tried to impose upon me, it was very distressing and I started rambling on about all sorts of things but I eventually said no. What happened then was that I was immediately surrounded by the energy of the attempted rape, I was in it completely.

Reflecting upon this again I saw that every time that someone tried to impose something upon me with no regard to my boundaries and tried to step into my personal space without my permission I was reliving the energy of what had taken place. We do this without the realisation of it, we continuously relive painful experiences and the people who provide these teachings are enabling us to heal this pattern, they are our teachers.

I had no boundaries and my mother used to say to me that I would give myself away and I allowed everyone in and I know now from what I have just gone back to reclaim that it goes back to the time when I was 21 where someone entered my sacred space and crossed my boundaries.

However as in all things we often go from one extreme to the other and after the lady in question died subconsciously I tightened my boundaries so that no one would ever again disrespect them but I went too far and they became so tight I wasn't being my normal loving self.

The friend who gave me the message this past week gave me another message at that time and she saw spikes all over my head and the head represents your thoughts and I had become spiky, I had created the spikes as my protection so that no one would step through my boundaries, to be truthful I was terrified that anyone would try to get in again in the way that lady had.

It is understanding which heals us and through my understanding of the spikes upon my head I realised what I had done so I made the journey back to my normal gentle loving self but my boundaries are still strong and I have no fear that anyone will cross them and all I need now is a simple no.

Symbolism is the greater part of my work and this is what I teach and there is so much magic in working in this way. The very day when I received this message last week from my friend and I sat in the garden and worked with it and had realisations and brought back my light some men had come to chop down a large cherry tree in our front garden. It was very sad but necessary as the roots were lifting up the path but here is the magic because as soon as I stepped into the living room I wondered where all the light was coming from, it was flooded with light. I had not realised how much the cherry tree had been blocking the light. Graham and I are still amazed that our bungalow is filled with incredible light now. How amazing is that, the light of true understanding.

Someone is coming to grind the roots next week so that will be a further healing for me as I delve deeper into a greater understanding of the roots of myself.

One wonderful more symbol happened that same afternoon as we discovered we have a hedgehog living in our garden and hedgehogs haven't been here for years and years. As I looked upon it with its spines flat against its body it reminded me of how I had been spiky to protect my boundaries and it was a wonderful symbol for me for those a spikes had served a purpose for me to protect me but I no longer needed them and they have long gone.

With all that you have experienced whatever it is even if you think you have healed these things go back and find what you have left there, the part of you which is still there and bring back your light. Bring it back and feel the difference within you and it will put the light of greater understanding on all that you have gone through.

Shine bright and claim your light and let it shine for the whole world to see.

Glastonbury

Graham and I have just returned from spending a fabulous time in Glastonbury but a week before we went away I hurt my foot and I have no idea how this had happened physically but I understood what had happened on an energetic level. It did not deter us and so I hobbled around Glastonbury and we visited all the usual sites and thoroughly enjoyed our time spent there.

Usually when we go away we explore the place and then Graham will relax and I go out roaming. I love to roam the lanes and the fields in Glastonbury and I can be out for hours but this time it was different. We were staying in a beautiful cottage at the foot of the Tor with our own Tor Gate, our private entrance onto the Tor so instead of my roaming I sat on the lower field at the bottom of the Tor.

I thoroughly enjoyed sitting there facing Chalice Hill and watching the mists of Avalon as the day drew to a close. I would even go back to the cottage and get changed for going out to dinner earlier than usual and then go back and sit and watch the sunset.

We had such a wonderful time in Glastonbury enjoying all its magic and its eccentricities. Graham overheard two men talking by the market cross and they were talking about a woman who was a survivor of an illuminati attack and then when he went to the health food shop to buy arnica for my foot a fight nearly broke out there in the queue between those wearing masks and those who were not wearing masks. It is all part of the colour of this wonderful place.

I bathed my foot in the healing pool at the Chalice Well and I used the arnica but it was not those things which helped to bring me healing it was an experience I had as one evening I hobbled back to the cottage and a lady walking up the Tor path stopped me and she asked if I had hurt my foot. She went on to tell me she had hurt her foot also. She was a most unusual person and there were things about her which were certainly not ordinary. She told me she had hurt her foot because she had had a thorn in it. When she went to go on her way she shouted to me, bless you.

Everything in life is a mirror and every ailment we create ourselves and that very special lady was a mirror to me so I knew that energetically I had a thorn in my foot. I also knew by my observation of her and how she appeared that Jesus was speaking through her, I have no doubt about that.

I sat and I removed the thorn in its energy form as I reflected on its meaning. When my foot first became sore something someone had said to me had upset me and in that moment I froze and I stopped the flow of energy within me because I wasn't very pleased. I had a further confirmation of this because when it happened I had a vase of flowers on the window sill and I asked my higher self what was causing the pain in my foot and in that very moment a rose in the vase which is called Margareta, my name, jumped out of the vase onto the windowsill. This told me that I had stopped the flow and I was out of the water and I needed to be back in the flow, back in the water. This is all about energy. As I healed my foot and transformed the energy of the thorn which I had pulled out energetically from it I realised that I had been spiky in my thoughts so my energy became stuck and gathered around my foot.

The foot carries much symbolism, it is about our roots and it also carries the sole which is symbolic of the soul.

As I carried out the healing I suddenly remembered a message a friend had given me several months before and the message was that I was to watch where I would walk in case I stood on something hard and I would hurt my foot and I would only really be hurting myself. This is all symbolic. I had stood on something hard and I hardened and stopped the flow. I then remembered who had brought that message to my friend for me and it was Jesus and he had warned me and he came back through that lady on the path to the Tor to remind me.

Glastonbury worked its magic again and I met someone very special through that unusual lady and this reminds us that we never really know who we are talking to or who is working through them. I knew I had created the pain in my foot and I knew I had stopped myself moving forward, I had done it to myself. We are responsible for ourselves and physical pain is a message about the inner pain we experience when we hold on to old emotions. There is nothing out there which causes your problems, not the moon, not ascension energies no matter what anyone might tell you, it is our own selves which create our problems and our bodies are our teachers.

Glastonbury is like nowhere else, I love the place, I love the peace, I love how people smile and speak to you and the kindness there and I love how it is a place where everyone can just be themselves which is the greatest magic of all.

The Spirit Of Healing

Everything has a spirit and everything is part of spirit and everything has consciousness; there is nothing which does not have consciousness, all things of heaven and earth are alive with spirit.

What this means is that the spirit of all manner of things can come to you, for example, the spirit of truth or the spirit of freedom or the spirit of understanding, you can be visited by all these things and much more. I remember years ago when the spirit of understanding came to me and I didn't understand or recognise who it was. It appeared before me as a column of golden shimmering light and I later discovered that this was the spirit of understanding or the light of understanding. I was able to communicate with it and now when it comes to me it comes as a being of golden light as real as any of the great teachers.

If you can feel into this with the knowledge that you can communicate with the spirit of all things it opens up infinite possibilities. Begin this journey into new territory where you see that all things have consciousness even ideas and allow today the spirit of healing to appear to you. The colour of healing is blue and so the spirit of healing can come to you as blue light and with form.

This is a very powerful way to work with the light, I cannot emphasise how powerful it is. You are used to calling upon your teachers in the light and you call upon specific ones to bring their particular qualities and their particular healing but now take this a step further and call on the spirit of understanding when you need wisdom and call upon the spirit of healing when you need healing.

At this moment it is the spirit of healing which I can feel very much present today on a collective level. Let it come to you in form within the colour of blue and you can see it as either male or female for what you are working with is energy made manifest and it is the energy and the essence of healing.

Call the spirit to you and ask for their healing and feel their blue light fill you in whichever way they choose to bring it and sit within that light and receive that healing and know that it goes to the very core of you to help you in what ever way you need help.

This feels like a wave of energy available to you and more than anything on this day it is healing which makes its way into our lives. We heal ourselves in so many ways and we heal ourselves first and foremost through understanding, through self understanding but we can also receive the essence of healing for our bodies and minds.

Make friends today with the spirit of healing and its healing blue light which will fill every cell of your body and every thought in your mind and rejoice in the knowledge that you have been blessed by this visitation.

Call upon the spirit of healing again when ever you need it but also remember to call upon the spirit of anything at all for what ever you need. We forget sometimes that there is immense help waiting for us but we have to open the door to that help and reach out for it so let the spirit of all things enter into your life and watch and marvel at the miracles which will unfold for you.

Spiritual Tiredness

I have heard quite a few people mention recently that they are feeling tired. Some blame it on the energies and there are often many posts telling people that the energies which are present from spirit are causing their problems. This is not so for we always have to bring everything back to ourselves and not put the cause of what we are feeling onto what is outside of us.

There are several reasons why you can feel tired and here I am talking about energetic tiredness. If you have unresolved emotions within you and they are trying to come to the surface to be looked at it can become a very heavy weight to carry around; the energy of it is very heavy and it can make you physically tired.

Here is another reason; sometimes you are still working with old energy when there is new energy there for you. The old energy does not sit well with the new energy so you need to shift and move into the new.

There is another reason for feeling tired when you follow the spiritual path and that is if you are not using your energy fully it can remain around you and feel heavy as well and it can make you feel tired. As you grow spiritually your energy increases and your light increases and that light needs to be used and used for others. If you are not working on your full power then that energy can stay within you and that too can make you feel tired. All of these energies are like grey fuzzy blankets gathered around you.

What you need to do is to look and see whether an old emotion has been triggered and you can feel it trying to rise to the surface and if you are aware of this then work with it and transform it and you will have your energy back. If you are still held in the old but yet you are aware of the feeling of newness then you know that you have to make a shift and bring in the new in any way you can.

If you feel that you are not fully using all your light then use it in any way and you can particularly use it with the spoken word. You can use it in your healing and in the wisdom which you give out and if there is no one to work with then hold your hands out and send your light out into the world. Energies need to flow when they become stuck for they can make you very tired indeed so don't look to the outer world or to ascension energies making you tired or making you feel anything else look only to yourself.

A huge rainbow serpent came to me today and the ancients knew about the rainbow serpent for it is a symbol of the energies of the earth and the flow of energies for the earth contains many colours and we can receive those colours to renew us. Colours are so important in everything we do so connect to the rainbow serpent and make friends with him and ask him to share his colours with you and ask him to show you how to create flow in your life. Or put your feet upon the ground and ask mother Earth to bring her colours to you and feel them flowing through you. Walk amongst the flowers or visualise them and draw in their rainbow colours and by doing all these things you will immediately feel a complete change of energy. Our colours need changing daily.

The earth contains the rainbow within her and the rainbow serpent and its colours feed us helping us to renew our energies daily.

Synhronicities

Life is full of synchronicities and so much magic and there is a purpose to these things and they serve as a constant reminder that we are spirit beings living in a physical body in a physical existence and that behind everything there is always light and love.

As I write these words for you these words are filled with the brightest golden light for words carry vibrations within and they can heal those who read them. As you read this that light will fill you and it will bring you love, healing and peace. There is no distance between any of us we are all just a thought away and our souls can be in direct communication at any time.

I love synchronicities and even having witnessed so many I am still deeply amazed when they happen and they bring me so much joy and comfort letting me know that I am not alone and that there is a purpose to everything.

Graham and I recently visited South Shields in the north-east to spend time with my family and a couple of days before we went there Graham bought something on eBay and he asked me if I minded doing a detour on the way up there to collect his purchase but when he told me the name of the place I was most surprised. It was a small town in the Yorkshire Dales called Bedale but it also happened to be the same place where my brother and his partner were staying the night before they continued on to South Shields from where they live part of the year in Cambridgeshire. What this meant was that we had a wonderful opportunity to spend some extra time with both of them and it was an absolute delight. My brother spends a good part of the year in America and because of the lockdown he has had to stay in England but I haven't seen him for a year so I was over the moon to have some extra time with him and his partner.

I have witnessed so many coincidences, I remember once when visiting my brother in California and we went to a pub one evening where I met a man who was brought up in the next road to where I lived. We were about the same age so we had grown up in the same place. All these things are to let us know that there is a guiding hand behind everything and that there is a purpose and that purpose is to show us that we are not alone.

Many years ago long after my divorce from my first husband and after I had married Graham I received an email from my ex-husband who I hadn't heard from since we separated and he must have found my email address on the Internet. I knew he wasn't well because someone had told me and I knew that he did not have long to live. The strangest thing was that the day before I received his email I had been to a lavender farm in Lancashire with Graham and in Alan's email he too had been there the day before.

Coincidences are all part of a greater plan even if they do not have much meaning but they are there to show us that life is not all that it seems and beyond everything there is a greater purpose and there is always love and light.

In the same way behind these words which you are reading there is love and light and you will receive that love and light and it will bring you peace and healing. Beyond everything including these words is a vast ocean of light guiding you and holding you always.

15 months after writing the above post I will now add a little extra. I described how Graham and I had met my brother in a village called Bedale in Yorkshire and I knew that it was more than a coincidence that we were in the same place on our travels to the north-east of England. I knew my brother wasn't well but I did not know how serious it was and yet at the same time I also knew that I was given this extra opportunity to spend time with him, time just for us. I knew it without a doubt and I also knew that I would look back in the

future and see how precious these moments were. I felt it in the depths of my being.

He passed away less than a year after that meeting and I treasure my memories of our time spent together in Bedale.

The Buddha Speaks

The room that I work in has Buddha wallpaper on the walls and the other evening I noticed that a rainbow from the crystal hanging above the patio doors was shining directly into the mouth of one of the pictures of the Buddha. It was extraordinary to see this because it looked as though the Buddha was speaking and producing rainbows.

Buddhas are often associated with rainbows and when they die very often rainbows can be seen surrounding their body. It is from this where we have understood about the diamond rainbow light body for we can call the soul the diamond rainbow light body.

Whenever a Buddha in spirit comes to work with you they bring peace, enlightenment and stillness and they always teach about the middle path which means that you never go to any extremes, you always stay in the middle.

Enlightenment is the goal of many who follow the spiritual path and the word actually means to be in the light and the light is truth and understanding. Enlightenment comes as a process and it comes from letting go and letting go again and again and no amount of meditation or spiritual practices will lead you there until you let go. The Buddha energy teaches us to just be, to find the stillness within, not reaching out for anything but just learning to be content in the moment.

The journey to enlightenment is all about the shedding of layer after layer to reveal the true you underneath and it is through this that you find yourself and come home. It is not about being immersed in the light it is about just being yourself and in that is infinite peace. Our front garden is only small and I do not tend to it as I put all my energy into the back garden and I decided this year to let the four buddleias there grow wild and I planted different seeds amongst the paving stones. It is interesting that the buddleia is symbolic of the Buddha. I went out yesterday to water the little rockeries which I have there and as I stood in the sunlight in the wildness of it the most incredible peace came over me.

As this garden had been untouched for most of this year the energy had not been disturbed and as I basked in it there was perfect peace within it. Later on I contemplated that energy and I went back into it and I was shown that what I had experienced was the energy of my soul. It is interesting because my passion is nature and so to reveal my soul to me as a wild place fits me so well. I brought that energy back again so I was completely enveloped in the peace of my soul which I can only describe as a wild untouched place in nature and it was incredibly beautiful.

What I had been shown in the garden was my Buddha self for the Buddha self is the higher part of us and I was shown what it is like when you rest in your soul and just be.

So connect to your Buddha self and let your soul be revealed to you, your diamond rainbow light body. I realise now that the Buddha on the wallpaper was waiting to show me this experience but his message is for everyone that the peace that you seek and the enlightenment comes from letting go and what people often speak of as letting god goddess in is the realisation that you are god goddess and all that you seek is within you.

Enlightenment

This journey upon the spiritual path is one of
becoming and the becoming is the becoming more of
who you really are. Enlightenment is not a state of
walking in bliss it is about coming home to yourself
and becoming very ordinary.

How many times in your life have you wished you
were not as you are or you may have felt ashamed of
the way you are and you have listened to other people
who have put you down or criticised you; all of these
things pushed the real you down deep inside.

However there comes a day when you can no longer
squash down you and you open the door and let
yourself out and allow yourself to be seen for who you
really are.

I hear this time and time again of how people feel
shame for how they are, how they feel not good
enough, of how they have been criticised because of
their spiritual ways and of how they do not feel as
good as other people. Let me tell you now that you are
as good as anyone else you are just different and it is
your uniqueness which you need to celebrate.

No matter what people have said to you or how they have put you down and no matter how often you have believed them make your mind up that you will only now believe in yourself. Look at all those things within yourself that you feel shame with whether these are physical attributes or emotional ways of being and tell them that they are part of you and it is these things which make you as you are.

In this moment make your mind up to accept yourself and every part of you and tell yourself that you are as good as anyone else and also tell yourself that your uniqueness and different ways of being are beautiful for why would you want to be like anyone else. Many of you have been criticised by others for your spiritual ways but others just don't understand so accept your ways even more.

We have a foot in the world and a foot in the world of spirit and we have to be fully grounded and present here at the same time as being aware that there are other realities all around us and we need to always create balance. We can converse with other people about ordinary things and love them for who they are but it is our spiritual friends who feed us and accept us and that is why it is so important to surround yourself with people like yourself.

Fill yourself up with crystalline light the moment you read this and let it flow through you as a river of light to shine in all those places which you do not accept, shine the light so bright and see how special you really are and if you are different from most people then that is truly a blessing. I love people who are unique and do their own thing. Miriam Margolyes is presently in a television series about Australia and I have written about her before because she inspires me so much. She doesn't care what people think about her, she swears like a trooper, she asks all sorts of questions of people but she has such a huge heart and an unquenchable thirst for life with a great interest in everyone she meets. She speaks her mind and she is not afraid to be herself.

We are all just becoming and in that becoming just like Dorothy in the Wizard of Oz we find our way back home discovering the truth that home is here and it always has been and when we come home to ourselves we can celebrate our uniqueness and love ourselves all the more for it.

Blossom And Bloom

We can learn so much from nature as she has much to teach us. The old healers of the past learned much from observing nature and reading the signs and all the ancient cultures understood this language as well. This is the language of light, the true language of light, the language of spirit. All traditional Chinese medicine comes from the observation of nature and the wisdom which comes from understanding the changing of the seasons.

All it needs to receive guidance and teachings is to be aware and to listen with the heart and to trust what you feel when you are being called by a plant or a bird or a stone and the riches which you will receive from this direct communication will bring you everything you need.

I have some pink snapdragons which I bought last year and they appeared again this year, I find that these flowers will often return again even though they are only supposed to flower for one season. They were absolutely tremendous and they bloomed and they brought me so much pleasure. If you cut down some flowers after they have flowered if you are fortunate they will flower a second time for you and the other day I found that my snapdragons had decided to flower again. As always this brings me such joy in my heart to see the return again of old friends. There is so much we can learn from the garden, we do not have to travel far to observe the wisdom of nature and what the snapdragons were teaching me was that when we cut things back they return and often even stronger and better.

In our lives there are times when we need to cut back and by doing this we create a clearing. That clearing can be removing clutter from your home, cutting down on your activities or even stepping back from certain people in your life, it is all clearing and every now and then we need to cut back on the old so that the new can come in.

There is a saying, every day I grow new wood and to grow new wood we need to prune and prune ourselves, prune the things around us but also our old thoughts and ways of thinking. The new cannot come in until the old has released. Sometimes it takes courage to cut things back and to say no and to spend time just being with yourself and doing what you love and what is right for you but the rewards are enormous. It is in those times when you are cut back to the ground where you grow the most because you spend time with you reflecting upon your past and discovering where you need to go.

If you have been feeling that you have had to cut back on much in your life or that you still need to cut back on even more then just follow your feelings and go with it and know that like the snapdragons you will bloom and blossom again so allow the old to go and create space for the new to enter.

My Garden

Sometimes I invite people to come into my garden in spirit, in the light and I am inviting you now today to come and join me whenever you wish if you need healing and peace.

Our gardens are filled with our own vibrations and these build up in time and because I have worked for the last 20 years not only in creating our garden but also I have sat outside and worked with myself and with many teachers so this space is filled with wonderful energies. I have also worked with the elemental beings and the flowers and trees and the insects and the birds and because of all of this communication there is much light here in our garden. I have experienced much healing for myself personally and I have shed many tears as I released whatever needed to be released but I have also been immersed in the joy and the light of the continual presence of those who have come to help me. Many teachers have graced this garden, bringing teachings which I share with others and so the light is passed on continuously.

The garden is filled with peace and also with all the love which we have put into it over the years so come and join me whenever you need some comfort or some healing or a reassuring helping hand whether it is day or night and sit in the peace which is always here.

You can come and join me as I once again share my garden with you. There are flowerbeds filled with my favourite cottage garden flowers, I do not like exotic flowers I only like the more natural ones. I have a bed for my herbs with all my favourite ones in there and my most favourite of all is lovage which smells like celery and grows very tall. My favourite place to sit is behind the shed where I have created a sacred space with many flowers and roses and the climbing clematis which carries my name, Margaret Hunt.

I also have a beautiful fairy house here specially crafted for me by a friend who put so much into it. I have a statue of the Green man, a hare, a statue of St. Francis and some fairies here plus the birdbath so that I am always close to the birds who sing in the trees beyond. The other side of the garden is lined by elder trees with huge popular trees overhanging and it is here where I have created a new flowerbed to house my recent addition of a beautiful goddess statue. I planted a pink rambling rose behind her called Awakening and she was at home the moment I placed her there.

At the bottom of the garden is my fairyland which I often write about. I have an arch there covered in a pink rose and a white rambling rose and there is a little path which leads to a seat where it is all overgrown. I have crystals hanging in the trees, the sun and moon and many other things which people have gifted me and red and white toadstools on the ground and a lovely statue of Merlin. Just next to fairyland is an old gate which leads out to the trees beyond and to the little river which I walk along and there is an old pink rose which grows over the doorway.

So come and join me whenever you wish and sit with me in fairyland or behind the shed and we will share the gossip and drink endless cups of tea and eat home-made cake for as long as we wish and if you need healing I will put my hand on yours and let you know that everything will be all right.

We can sit there in the sunshine accompanied by the insects and the bees and birds and we can sit there at night under the moon and under the stars surrounded by moths and bats. There are times where a person will suddenly appear in my garden, they come in the soul state, it can be a friend who has come to say hello or it can be someone who has come who needs help so I invite you too to come and join me when you need comfort and reassurance and healing.

The Bees

On Thursday evening the bees came into the gathering
I was running and they brought their sacred sound,
their hum. Since then I have written about the bees and
other people have as well. The bees are calling us very
much; I even had one sitting on my plate as I was
enjoying some cake in the garden.

The bees are very sacred and there is so much that can
be written about them, from their sense of community
to their symbols like the honey, pollen, nectar, the
hexagon, the beehive shape but the bees bring more
than this. Like the birds they are the carriers of the
news and they always have much to share with us.
There were priestesses dedicated to the bees, the
Melissae, a long time ago and they would wear wings
and they would dance like the bees and there are
inscriptions of bees on temple walls in many places.
We are very aware of the bees and their importance at
this time and of how we need to conserve them but
they come to us at this moment to share their wisdom
with us. The queen bee, the queen bee spirit, is the total
expression of the bee kingdom and she has made

herself known, the great bee spirit who oversees the whole realm of bees and she wishes to speak to you.

Deep within you is a sacred sound for you are made of light and sound and this sound is the very fabric of existence and it can be heard when you turn very deeply inwards. It is the sound of the humming of the bees and there are those of you who know the technique of listening to this inner sound for it has been known since ancient times and knowledge of it has been passed down from teacher to student.
This sound permeates the universe and from it and from the light which accompanies it all matter has manifested. If you sit quietly and go deep within and listen you might hear it too. Listening to this sound or chanting it will bring you into communion with everything which exists for you will be connecting to the sound which permeates all things.
This sacred sound this humming is the same sound which also connects you to Mary Magdalene and if you chant it you will vibrate with her energy also. Take the letter M and let it flow from you and keep repeating it and you will soon discover that you are immersed in the vibration of the divine feminine as brought to you at this time by Mary Magdalene and

also by the queen bee, the bee spirit who presides over the bee realms.

Feel how quickly this sound vibrates within and brings you calm and peace and you will then discover that the greatest gift of all which the bees bring to you is the ability to just be. To accept your life as it is and of all it has been and of all it is now, accepting it in its completeness and then you will find that you can just be.

So take this sound and let its vibration fill you completely and you will learn how easy it is to just be.

My Goddess Self

My sister recently sent me some old photographs and amongst them was one of myself 25 years ago. It was not long after my divorce from my first marriage and it was a few months before I met Graham. I was living in a rented stone cottage which I loved but it had damp running down the walls and a tree trunk in the cupboard under the stairs. I had gone without a garden for two years after living in a basement flat and after leaving the home I had shared with my husband but at last I had a garden again; I was in my element.

My cat Rosy was delighted as well and she would often stroll in through the back door of the pub opposite my garden, she was in her element too. It was during this time when I had friends from America staying with me and we decided to have some fun so I dressed up as Madame Mag and we got the cards out and the cigarettes. The cigarettes along with many other things are long gone but I can still look back to the joy of the time and it was wonderful to see this photograph again.

I have many happy memories from living in that cottage where people would squeeze in to the tiny front room for spiritual groups and there were often other spiritual gatherings until the small hours of the morning. The air was thick not only with cigarette smoke but also with much laughter. Close friends came for dinner and left with the milkman and there was rarely a day or should I say evening without people being there to share spirit.

For all of us who follow the spiritual path we are also on our own personal healing path and as we dig deeper we go over the past to reveal those things which caused us emotional pain and we have to return to those occasions many times over to complete the healing. I'm sure that many of you reading this have had emotional pain to deal with and the memories still come back to you and indeed the patterns which created them might still be present however there have always been happy times and happy memories. Often when we are working so deep to clear the emotional body we forget to bring to our memory those things which brought us joy.

Living in my little cottage carried its own healing and I had much to heal within but I can look at this photograph and remember all the laughter and all the things I used to get up to with sharing time with wonderful friends and there would always be someone who would give you a reading. I enjoyed my outings roaming down the lanes and in the park often coming back with an acquired bunch of flowers which brought me the greatest joy.

So I share this with you today to remind you to remember the happy times and all the joy and all the friends and all the laughter you have experienced in your life and this will bring in a beautiful balance and a wonderful healing. Reflecting back on that picture I can see that I am still the old hippie and I always will be, I will always wear bright clothes and I will always go out roaming in wild places. Remember your joys and acknowledge the truth of you and who you always have been and of whom you always will be and you too may find that you as well have a hippie heart.

I will just add to this that the other day I was in the garden and I said to spirit show me my goddess self and at that very moment Graham called me into the house and showed me a parcel which had just been delivered. I opened it and found the most wonderful gift from him. It was a pair of vegan flowery Doc Marten's. When I tried them on he said they are just you and how right he was.

The Blackbird

Since early spring a male blackbird has come to keep me company in the garden all day long. Each day he has sung his beautiful chorus so loud and so clear. He perches in the wild plum trees just by where I sit and he has become a good friend to me but it won't be long before the birds go quiet again as they retreat into the woods.

I always make the most of the birdsong at this special time as I know there won't be many days left where I am blessed by such wonderful singing but what a long season it has been this year and never have I heard so much delightful song.

The blackbird has always been a great friend of mine, he came both times when my mother passed and my father passed and in the months after the death of my mother a female blackbird accompanied me every day in the garden.

The blackbirds have come to tell me in the past when it was time to move for they have always been such wonderful messengers. The birds have much to teach us and they bring their own language, they bring the language of light as it has been known for a very long time. This is not the same as the light language which some people use now this is actually the interpretation of the language of the birds of the things that they do and the messages that they bring to us through direct observation of them.

The ancient ones would always instinctively know what the birds were telling them for they had such a deep connection to the bird realm. Of course our relatives and our teachers can come as birds as well to work with us for we do not have to see those in spirit in only human form. Birds have always been seen like the angels and the fairies as bringing a lighter energy and the ability to soar high and to see with great clarity of vision.

The song of the blackbird is very precious indeed and to me it is the finest song of all and I often turn to my companion in the garden and bow to him in recognition of all that he brings to me. He sings into the night until well after 10 o'clock and his singing often has never stopped throughout the day. I have appreciated this so deeply for birdsong brings us such elevated energy with its heavenly sounds.

Today I saw five goldfinches on the telephone wires and I knew what they were bringing for the goldfinches bring the gold and they always bring more wisdom. Each bird brings its own medicine and its own message, they bring the colours and they bring us guidance through whatever they do.

Make the most of the birds while they are still here visible to us before they take their leave for a little while, enjoy their evensong and their dawn chorus and talk to them and ask them for the news for the birds always bring the news but most of all give thanks to them not only for their beauty but for the beauty of their song.

The birds teach us one more thing and that is how to use our voice and to speak loud and clear and not to hold back and they also teach us to sing our own song which means to follow our own heart and to choose our own way of being and to find the freedom in doing so. So sing your own song and love yourself for this and even if others do not like your song that is up to them so give yourself the freedom to sing loud and clear.

The Crystal

Yesterday when I was in the garden I had my phone in my hand and suddenly the sun was reflected on the glass but what was most remarkable were two rainbowlike wings at either side of the Sun in the reflection, it was incredibly beautiful. Then this morning when I was looking at a multifaceted clear crystal I have hanging in a tree and there was no sunshine but the crystal was filled with rainbows, all the facets had rainbow colours in them.

These are soul energies as we connect to our soul and the purpose of our spiritual journey is to renew that connection and become at one with ourselves, this is the sacred marriage. It is a very lengthy journey and it is done in stages and it is a very great achievement if you actually get to that point within yourself.

You achieve this through the clearing after clearing of the emotional body and then eventually the lost parts of you can come together as one. This does not mean that the healing within stops because it never stops for we just go deeper and deeper into the understanding of ourselves and the letting go, this is a lifelong process.

The sun with wings which I saw and the faceted crystal are both symbols of the soul and the soul is like a crystal with many facets. We have many facets of ourselves, all the gods and goddesses are within us, they are part of us and as we claim the different aspects of ourselves we reclaim our god and goddess self once more.

Each facet of the crystal is a past life for we have lived many lives and deep within us we have all the wisdom we have learnt from each of these lives waiting for the time to come when that wisdom can be brought to the surface and acknowledged. Even though you may not feel that you are within your crystalline light and you may feel that you have a long way to go I would like to reassure you that that part of you is always present and it is your true reality. No matter what life brings to you, no matter what lessons you are learning and no matter how you may be struggling with different situations at the very heart of you you are still a multifaceted rainbow crystal filled with light. Never forget this.

If you are feeling a bit low or if you are feeling that you need to be energised and lifted up then manifest before you the multifaceted clear crystal and go and stand within it. Draw down the sunlight through you and through the crystal so that it lights up numerous rainbows of light. Stand within that light within the crystalline rainbow light and feel it filling you and bringing you everything which you need. Do this each day and it will connect you to your true self.

When you find yourself and when your soul is fully present you stand within your own power, knowledge and intuition and no-one can influence you because you are established in your own divine truth.

Draw in the crystalline light and fill yourself with rainbows and feel how quickly it can make a difference and lift you up and bring you hope, peace and the understanding that you are the most beautiful being of light and you always have been and you always will be.

Glastonbury Of The Heart

For many of you reading this Glastonbury will always be home and like me when you go there you really feel like you have arrived somewhere so special. Glastonbury is the heart centre of the world, the landscape there has been saturated with the essence of the goddess and the divine feminine and it is the place for the opening of the heart.

I have been to Glastonbury many times but during one of my earliest visits there I received a crystal heart into my heart as a gift. It happened one day as I was sitting outside the place we were staying with a view of the Tor and I watched as a beam of light descended from above and then radiated out towards me and within that light was a crystal heart.

There have been times when I have held workshops where I have given out crystal hearts to people because they always meant so much to me as a reminder of what I received in Glastonbury. We have travelled around the country providing workshops in the past including Glastonbury but we also held many as well in a village in North Wales called Cilcain and I chose this place because it was near to the sacred mountain of Moel Famau. The day we went to have a look at the village hall in Cilcain to see if it was suitable for a workshop we went to Moel Famau and as I stood on its slopes the mist came around me and I was very aware of roses with me as well and I was in Glastonbury and I knew that I had found Glastonbury and that sacred part of North Wales was to become Glastonbury for our work.

The last workshop we did in Glastonbury as we travelled home and came onto the Wirral where we live I turned to Graham and I said let us bring Glastonbury to the north and at that very moment a truck came up from behind and there written on the back of it was Glastonbury, Somerset.

The truth is that whenever we work from the heart we work in Glastonbury for its essence is the heart. We can create Glastonbury where ever we live and sit within all that it means; all that it represents but it is also one of the nicest things to do to go on an inner journey there. So take yourself to the Chalice Well Gardens there which are filled with peace and sit within them and absorb the vibrations. There is nothing you need to do only absorb the light and it will fill you from head to toe.

See yourself drinking water from the lion's head fountain in the garden and it will renew you, bathe in the bathing pool, go and sit in the meadow at the top of the garden where the wildflowers grow and take in all the peace. I know when I go there to the garden I don't want to leave because it just wraps its arms around you and holds you in its love and its light.

So visit there within and sit and feel the overwhelming calmness wash over you and let the healing vibrations heal all that needs healing and allow your heart to open and open to this blessed place and let it soothe your soul for indeed it does touch your soul to its very depths.

Beautiful Bride

The spiritual journey is the journey to the self and to the finding of self love but it goes far deeper than you can ever imagine and there is more to self love than you originally realise.

I have the most beautiful flowering clematis with a huge white flower called beautiful bride and it is in full flower. Graham has been parking his car in front of it and for several days I was very aware of the flowers reaching out to me and communicating with me, there was a feeling of them feeling neglected even though I often went to admire than. Then one day while Graham was out I could see the flowers in all their glory and I was drawn to stand before them and really take a good look at them.

The flowers then communicated with me and told me that what I was seeing was a reflection of my own soul for the soul is the bride, the name of the flower is a symbol of the other part of us for we have within us the bride and bridegroom and our spiritual path is about the sacred marriage of the union within. I stood and gazed for ages receiving constant feedback from the flowers repeating to me that what I was looking at was a reflection of my own soul and of how beautiful it really was with all my fears and for me to fully feel this.

I then had revelations about what we see as self love. Everything you are dealing with, every emotional problem and even most of your physical problems come from a lack of self love for if you have loved yourself you would not have put yourself through things, you would not have allowed the things you have allowed, you would have been in charge of your emotions and they would not have affected your physical body.

I pondered this, knowing that through everything I have experienced I have learnt to love myself but in that moment I knew that there was far more to this and the beautiful flowers were showing me a further truth. Through our spiritual awakening we learn our lessons and we learn to speak out to say no and to do the things which we really want to do and not be controlled by others but there is more to it. It is not enough to learn self love for there is also a deeper love which belongs to the soul, the greater part of you.

It is not enough to know that you love yourself; you need then to fully accept who you are. You need to accept that you are beautiful as you are and to accept your fears and instead of always feeling that you have to overcome them, that is not the answer, the answer is to accept them. You can strive and strive to face your fears but sometimes you are not able to face them you just cannot do it at that time and it is in those moments where you can then say, I accept this. You can accept your inability to do the things which you think you should do for in truth all you need to accept is that this is the way you are and you are beautiful with that and you love yourself even more for it.

So I share this with you so that in your journey to find self love you also find some acceptance and not feel that you need to constantly strive to overcome and to face your fears and to be the person you think you should be for all you need to be is yourself with the full acceptance of who you are. Love yourself and love your fears and just know that they are your teachings, such rich teachings to bring you self-knowledge and they have brought you to where you are now and even if you never ever in this life time face your fears accept them and love yourself for having them and then your soul will be very happy indeed.

The Centre

In the very centre of your garden there is a power spot and the same applies to your home. I often stand in the very middle of the lawn to receive energy from the Earth and from the heavens; you can do the same and if you do not have a garden then go to the central point in your home.

One day last week I moved my garden chair as it was too hot where I was sitting and when I looked I realised I had moved it to the very centre of the garden. As I sat there I was aware of a pool of liquid gold beneath me and I knew I had to take it in.

The next day I saw a huge clear crystal in that same spot and I knew that the elemental beings had brought it for me and so I drew that in as well.

The following day as I was busy mowing the lawn I turned and saw a huge chalice filled and overflowing with sparkling water. Eventually the chalice transformed into a fountain of the same sparkling water. All of these energies were being brought to me for me to use. I returned to that point again in the garden and as I did I watched as the golden pool blended with the clear quartz crystal and also with the water from the fountain to make the most radiant golden crystal water and I took that in also.

There are energies all around us, unseen energies if we only take the time to look and trust in what we see and remember that seeing is sensing and feeling, we see with the heart not with the eyes. These energies are the vibrations for you to use for your own healing and for you also to interpret your own messages and direction from.

Go to the centre of your garden or your home and go deep into the quietness and see and draw in the golden crystal water and let it flow through you. Let it go to those places where you have pain or discomfort and let it go to your heart and mind to bring you harmony. Watch as this flowing liquid flows up and out of your crown and up to the heavens creating a constant flow of light.

When you have done this you will feel that energy within and you can sit with it and allow it to bring you what ever you need illuminating everything for you so that you see more clearly than before.

Remember to return to the central point again and again so that you can fill up whenever you feel the need. The central point is called the Tai Chi and it also represents your centre, which is the deepest part of you and who you truly are.

Mary Magdalene

Many of you understand the truth of Mary Magdalene and you also have your own truth regarding her but some of you may not fully understand about her and so I am writing this post to share some insights with you. As with all things always trust your own intuition, only accept what feels right for you and if it doesn't feel right you will feel it in your heart.

What I share here may not be the same as what other people share for we all have our own way of receiving truth and truth is very much an individual thing.

Mary Magdalene's presence has been so strong in the last eight years; she is the bringer of not only love and the awakening of the divine feminine but she also brings truth. She comes to give you your voice back, a voice which has been silenced amongst many women and men, the voice of the divine feminine, the intuition which resides within.

Mary Magdalene was married to Jesus and they had three children. Jesus did not die on the cross, he was revived with healing herbs and ancient methods but there came a point where he and Mary Magdalene had to part and they went their separate ways.

Magdalene fled to Southern France due to the political unrest where she lived. She arrived by boat with her companions at Saintes Maries de la Mer in the Camargue and from there she spent time in the Languedoc and after that in Provence where she died. Sarah travelled with her and many say that she was her daughter but Sarah was actually the sister of Jesus and Magdalene's daughter was called Tamar.

There is an ancient tradition in Saintes Maries where people remember the one they call Sarah the Gypsy because she often travelled to Egypt from France and it was from that journeying that she received her name the Gypsy for the word Gypsy comes from the word Egyptian. She was called Sarah the Black as well because like Mary Magdalene she wore the black cloak of the Nazarene priestess.

Mary Magdalene was a very powerful person in her own right and she had her own followers even at the same time as Jesus taught his followers. The church eventually called her a prostitute to disempower her but this was a lie and its true purpose was to take away her status. Even some of the Apostles would not accept and treat her as an equal as she was a woman and they were jealous of her.

She did not come from an ordinary family and neither did Jesus for both were from royal lineages, Mary

Magdalene's father was a high priest. Magdalene carried the ancient teachings within her and in her ministry she not only taught and healed but she also performed baptisms. She was highly venerated when she lived in southern France even by royalty.

So we can understand why her presence is so strongly felt now for this is the time for nurturing, intuition and truth to rise up more than ever and this is what she brings to us. Many are now finding their voice again particularly women but there are still many who are afraid to be completely themselves to speak their truth and not be controlled by others. If you find it difficult to own your voice completely, then claim it back now no matter what the consequences, call upon Magdalene for this is what she is helping everyone with. If you are not familiar with her and with her true story then just know she is the ultimate expression of a free female, she is powerful and yet she is so gentle and loving. She lived a human life not just a spiritual life and so did Jesus so let all the myths about both of them shatter into the dust of the past; they were ordinary people as well as carriers of the ancient wisdom teachings so see them in their true light.

If you were not fully acquainted with Mary Magdalene before then let these words sink in and call her to you if you need to live in your own truth and if you need love for her love is so fierce and strong and powerful and she will hold you in it always.

Bee Balm

One of the most powerful herbs you can grow in your garden is lemon balm. It is a wonderful herb very good for your immune system but it is also wonderful for bringing relaxation.

Spiritually it brings the lemon which is the same as the gold and so it brings you the golden light of understanding. The tea made from the leaves is delicious and you can use fresh leaves or dried leaves. This herb is also known as Melissa which means bee balm. The bees love the little flowers upon it but the word bee also refers to priestesses.

In ancient times in the Mediterranean area and in certain other parts of the world there were bee priestesses who dedicated themselves to the bees. The bees are incredibly powerful healers and they carry much symbolic knowledge within them.

So when you drink a cup of lemon balm tea you are drawing in all these qualities and also the medicine of the bees.

I was given a small plant of this many years ago and since then it has seeded everywhere in my garden so once planted you are never without it. If you don't

have this herb then visualise it and see yourself
making a healing tea from it.

Truth

Whether you call him Jesus, Christ or Jeshua when he comes around you or when you work with his vibration you are working with the purest love, light and truth. He is the healer of hearts and Mary Magdalene is the queen of hearts for they both come to transform this centre of love.

When Jesus comes he brings truth and truth is one of the hardest things that we have to learn on this path to healing and awakening.

So many of you myself included have had to work so hard to find your voices for they have been quietened in your earlier life where you often gave your voice away and forgot what it was like to be able to speak the truth without any recriminations.

Whenever Jesus comes to work with you he will speak the truth through you and he will go straight to the heart of the matter with another person. His presence is very strong at this moment and if you turn to him you will feel him. From all your past suffering you learnt not to speak the truth because it would lead to rejection and anger and you weren't strong enough to answer back. I know that I wasn't strong enough in my past and it was all through fear.

The time has come to allow what Jesus stands for to be fully present in your life so that you speak the truth and you will know in your heart that it was right that you spoke the truth but what is different now is that maybe before when you were outspoken you felt guilt and doubt afterwards but now there can be no doubt or guilt just an inner knowing that it was right that you spoke as you did.

The throat chakra has probably been the most damaged chakra with most people for so much has been held in there and caused so much damage but now allow yourself to be free to speak out. Sometimes we say things to other people and then we immediately feel that we should not have but even if others cannot accept your truth somewhere they will have received the energy of your words. How can other people grow as well if they do not receive the truth? When someone is suffering deeply they need comfort and reassurance and love but very often they also need the truth and remember that this is the highest form of unconditional love. You love someone when you give them your truth for they cannot move on and heal without it. Only understanding can truly heal.

When Jesus was alive he was outspoken, he spoke his truth, he got angry and he did not hold back, he went right to the heart of anything and this is what he brings to you. You may be used to working with him with his gentle and loving ways but now allow his truth to pour through you and very often when he brings truth it is done with great directness. It is important when you deliver a message to someone that you give the energy of it along with the words for the energy will be received by a person to help them. See Jesus as he truly is; the healer of hearts, the light bringer but also the truth giver and more than any other teacher you will ever work with he is symbolic of truth.

Let his truth move through you and speak your truth and do not be afraid of it and do not be afraid of any recriminations for you have suffered for too long by not owning it and speaking it. You cannot go back to that place so speak loudly and clearly and have no fear of how others may react for that is their problem it is not yours. If they reject you because of what you say then that is all right; all that matters is that your throat centre is wide open and you no longer hold in your words.

Let Jesus come to you today with the truth and speak your truth like never before and you will set yourself free.

The Hawthorn

The hawthorn trees are abundant with red berries now so connect to them in person or in your inner journeying and receive their magic and their medicine. The berries contain the five pointed star, the mark of the goddess, on the end of them and so this is the goddess tree. Hawthorn berries carry much medicine for the heart but you do not need to take the actual medicine just connect to the berries and the tree itself and ask for healing. See yourself sitting beneath the tree and let the berries fill you with their healing essence whether you need healing for your physical heart or your emotional heart.

Let this wonderful tree soothe your heart and bring you healing, nurturing and love.

The Pink Dandelion

I have grown some pink dandelions from seed and
they have flowered and they are very beautiful and
they are still flowering but now they are setting seed.
Yesterday I noticed the most beautiful dandelion seed
clock on one of them, it was exquisite. A dandelion
clock represents time amongst other things and so I
took the meaning from this as it was time for the pink
and that meant time for love.

Love heals.

You can actually use love to heal yourself and to heal
others instead of working with energies. You can go
into your body and love those parts which are causing
you problems. You can wrap love around a person or
around where they have problems. You do this purely
with love.

So it is time for love.

The Violet Heart

Yesterday while I was in the garden and out walking I was amazed at how many violets are now in flower, it was as though they had just appeared.

Please connect to the Violet to bring you what ever you need for this time.

The Violet is the flower for the heart for its leaves are heart shaped so place a Violet in your heart and it will take away your anxiety and it will soothe you.

The Violet also brings the Violet flame, the colour where negativity cannot exist so use the Violet flame or the Violet flower upon yourself, your home or upon anyone.

There is more to the Violet flower than we generally understand so when you connect to it it will bring you many teachings.

The Sun

Recently in my heart was placed a golden sun and this
sun shone out far and wide and I share this sun with
you.

Manifest it within your heart and then shine your light
out to others and this way the golden light of the sun
will continue to spread amongst everyone.

People talk about the great central sun and this is often
referred to as the centre of the Milky Way however the
true great central sun is the source of light in the
realms of spirit and I have been shown it today.

This great central sun on the higher realms is the
source of light and just as in ancient times people
thought that the sun was god because without it they
would have died it is the same with this great central
sun for without this source of light we cannot exist.

So take in the light first of all for yourself and then
shine it brightly everywhere.

Babaji

Babaji first became known after the publication of
Yogananda's Autobiography Of A Yogi a long time
ago and since then he has been looked upon as an
astonishing being. Some of you will know about him
and you may even have worked with him and others
may not have heard of him but it was he who asked
Yogananda to go to the west to take his teachings and
spread them.

Much has been written about Babaji and he has always
been a mystery for there have been so many different
stories about him. There have been other yogis who
have claimed to have been a reincarnation of him but
that is not correct, there have been stories that he was
born in southern India a long time ago and that is not
correct. There are those who have claimed to have met
him and written about their experiences but much of
what has been written about him is not the truth.

There are beings who at some point in their life attain
self realisation or god realisation where they know and
have the direct experience of the unity of all things and
they know that they are part of the divine. However
way beyond this comes Babaji for he was never born so

he can never die. He is the manifestation of the divine, the manifestation of consciousness or god made manifest. I do not like using the word god for I feel that it separates and I prefer to use the term divine to express the unformed unlimited ocean of consciousness from which everything has arisen. Babaji has often been called Christ-like and indeed he is but he is beyond Christ for he is form manifested from the formless, the personalised expression of the divine. Of all the books and articles I have read about Babaji there is only one which has the truth and it is by Yogiraj Gurunath Siddhanath who wrote the book, Babaji: The Lightning Standing Still; he had direct experience of Babaji and he was shown the truth of who he is.

There was a picture commissioned by Yogananda of Babaji which has never felt right to me but when it comes to connecting to a being such as this we can all have our own personal interpretation of how they appear to us. He has always been said to have long hair which is copper coloured like fire and his skin is golden and although he can take on different forms he often appears very youthful and I know he is very slim also but it is his eyes which tell of his divine origins. Much of eastern spirituality that we work with today came from the teachings which originated from Babaji and then from Yogananda a long time ago. If you wish to make contact with what you would call god, goddess or the divine then turn to him and sit within his light and the fire which he brings. From the moment he first came to work with me some years ago he brought the fire. The fire he brings is not only the fire of spirit it is the fire of the life force, the kundalini and the energies which make up who we are and he teaches us how to be in harmony with those energies within to create healing and greater awakening. More than anything he brings love and peace in the heart and the knowledge of unity. He is love; he is love incarnate for he is the highest source you can ever connect to. He tells us that we are all being fed so much with so many teachings now with the ability to share knowledge in these modern times but he asks that we now be fed from the divine light where knowledge and healing come from so go and sit with him and sit in his divine presence.

Past Lives

This healing journey which we are on is all about the clearing of the heart and the emotional body from situations you have experienced in this present life. There are roots in your past and in your childhood which have created the emotional patterns, patterns which have caused you pain and suffering. As healers it is our job to dig out the roots of these things within ourselves and within others and go back to the beginning when something was created. The emphasis is always on this life however there can come a time where the root of all your problems in a past life is shown to you.

Many people describe their past lives but not all of these experiences belong there. A lot of the time what people perceive as a past life is actually their own inner suffering from this life. If you are meant to be shown the origins in the past when the seeds of your emotional patterns were first planted it will come at the right time and not before for much clearing has to be done first.

I have cleared so much from my experiences in this life but I always knew there was something else something to see and I was fortunate this week to be shown what it was. I have always had to deal with fear but there came a point when I began to experience phobias and when the energies of them came over me it was completely overwhelming and complete terror, real pure terror. I have accepted my fear, my phobias and the terror because they have been my teacher and even though people not on the spiritual path would never begin to understand them they give me the compassion to understand others who live with fear or phobias.

Some years ago I was given a vision of what was done to me in a past life and it was so utterly terrifying but I felt it had been my imagination which had created it and so I told no-one about it. Then last Tuesday when I met a friend for lunch she told me that on her way to meet me she was shown that my phobia came from a past life and she described what had been done to me as a sacrifice and I was utterly amazed because what she described was what I had been shown myself some years ago.

When I was first shown this I looked and searched to find any ancient cultures which used such rituals during their sacrificial practices but I found nothing at all but now I have my confirmation. I had never spoken to another person about this before.

My friend gave me further few clues ones which I already had the feeling about. She saw the temple where the sacrifice took place and I knew it was in South America and I had a feeling of the Incas and yet I knew it went further back than them. There were pre-Incan civilisations in Peru and in fact there were civilisations there going back 10,000 years. I knew that that life was thousands upon thousands of years ago. When we are ready to see something the universe conspires to bring us signs that we are on the right track and I saw lots of signs. Just before I went out to meet my friend I received some herbs from my herbalist and I should have received them a week ago but she had forgotten to send them and I told her not to worry as everything came at the right time. When I looked at the herbs, she had given me a new one and when I returned home I Googled it. It was a South American herb, the favourite herb used by the Incas. I knew I had already been familiar with this in that life. Just before I went out I put a new soap out one which I had made in the shape of a sunflower. I have long associated sunflowers with South America for they were classed as sacred and only royalty and priestesses could carry them.

That same morning when I woke up I saw a huge multicoloured bird, I received the teachings from it to share with those whom I help but I also had a feeling that it was Quetzalcoatl the great god of the Americas. When I googled him I saw that he was sacred to the Incas but he went under another name and he was always seen with feathers. So the clues were there. I decided to spend the next three days going within to make my connection to that life. Before I began a black butterfly fluttered towards me and I knew it was relevant. When I googled it it turned out that there is a Peruvian film called the black butterfly and it is about a murder.

During the next three days each time I would go within I was shown symbols and information and I looked up everything I received giving me more confirmation of what I was being shown.

I was shown that life and I saw myself walking up the steps of a temple way beyond any historical references and when I got to the top all I could feel was the sun and standing before me dressed in feathers was a priest. I later found out that the rulers were known as the sun or the son of the sun. I knew beforehand that this person was from this present life and I have always had a feeling that there was a connection to something with them which had happened in a previous life.

I looked into the eyes of this man and I recognised the eyes for they belonged to someone whom I had been greatly fearful of in the past in this present life. I am not to share with you the details of what took place but I was sacrificed in the most horrific way with a very slow death. The memory of that has followed me from every lifetime I have lived since then until this present life until the time when I was ready to see it and the life time where the priest who did this to me came back into my life again.

I have healed the roots of my emotional patterns in this life time but now I have been shown the ultimate root behind everything right back to the very beginning and I now know why I have phobias. This does not mean that those phobias will go away but hopefully in time with more understanding they may be healed but what is more important than anything else is that when the terrors comes again I can say that I know what it is and I can love that part of me which suffered so much so long ago.

I always share stories from my own life so that others can receive teachings from them and it is important that I share this with you so that you too can understand that what ever you go through it has roots way back in time. However you do not need to go into past lives to find these for you will not find them you will only discover them when your higher self and spirit recognise that it is time and they will bring you the information just as I was brought information. Everything conspires when the time is right to bring you healing; my herbalist did not realise that by sending me an ancient South American herb it would be part of the picture of what I was to be shown. I had also been told by my friend when the recent new moon came that there was something happening which would progress to the full moon. The full moon is in the morning and it just happens to be in my sign of virgo so the astrology is also perfect for the discovery of that life when the seed of my emotional trauma was first planted.

Lifetime after life time this has been within me and shaped the patterns of my emotional life but I just marvel at the synchronicity and perfection of life and of spirit and the knowledge that nothing can be given to you until it is time and that whatever you experience is always on time and it is always right. So just know that there is a higher force and a higher plan always working through you. I must add that this experience has not upset me in any way and I have no feelings of unforgiveness at all regarding the person who did this to me for everything is just perfect as it is meant to be.

A Mary Garden

A Mary Garden is a garden dedicated to Mary where the flowers contained within it are symbols of Mary herself.

Long ago monks and nuns meditated upon certain flowers which to them were symbolic of different aspects of Mary and so from this Mary Gardens were created. Every flower and every plant has its own signature which means its own particular vibration and if we delve deep into the essence of a flower we can receive information regarding its healing qualities. Each flower has its own plant spirit as well but they are also all connected to the great cosmic teachers for everything is about vibration and there are heavenly guides who vibrate on the same level as the flowers. Mary has long been associated with various flowers and so if you plant them in your garden you bring in the vibration of her.

We can expand upon our understanding of Mary and the whole aspect of what she means, she is the mother, the nurturer, the divine mother, the one who looks after us and in truth she is no different than the goddess. Christianity in trying to repress the goddess culture transferred the knowledge of the goddess on to Mary but for all of us who see the unity in all things we can understand that Mary the mother is also the goddess.

She is the great goddess whom we can turn to in times of need when we need nurturing and we need the unconditional love of a mother. The flowers dedicated to Mary are snowdrops, marigolds, rosemary, the madonna lily, columbine, daisies, lavender, violets, irises and many more. We can read about all these flowers and research them but the best way of all to understand the meaning of anything is to follow your own heart and listen to your own intuition and the guidance of your higher self and that way you find your own truth.

There are Mary Gardens where people can visit but you can create a corner in your own garden dedicated to the great mother and plant those flowers which are associated with her. It could be a tiny corner, a flower bed or even a flower pot and by doing this you will receive healing from your connection to the nurturing essence of these flowers.

Mary's ray is pale blue and so flowers of this colour belong to her but the pale blue is also the colour of the goddess for there is no difference. Let the flowers speak to you and learn their language and learn not only the healing properties which they bring but also discover those great teachers who come from the same vibration as them. Each flower is a realm in itself and its colour also will connect you to many other things and other beings.

When life is challenging very often you feel the need for nurturing and self nurturing is the greatest thing you can do but there are times also where we would all love a mother's arms around us and this is not always possible so connect to the great mother through your flowers and you will receive all the love, reassurance and nurturing that you need.

Happiness Is

Graham and I recently spent a night away in Llanrwst in the Conway Valley in North Wales for Valentine's day. We had booked a table for dinner in the only restaurant in the little town for the evening and after we had checked into our hotel we went to look for somewhere to have lunch. We couldn't find anywhere to eat but we discovered a chip shop and we thought it would be fun to go and buy chips and sit outside.

As soon as we came out of the chip shop it began to pour down and Graham pointed to a bus shelter ahead of us and so we sat in there and enjoyed a feast. We were very amused by what we were doing and then I remembered something. A few weeks after I had begun seeing Graham 24 years ago, on Valentine's day I was working in the evening and so he picked me up at lunchtime as a surprise and I didn't know where we were going. He took me to a beautiful place by the River Dee overlooking the Welsh hills and he had brought with him chips and champagne.

As we sat in that bus shelter we reminisced about our first Valentine's day together and of how similar it was to the present one and we reaffirmed something we have always said over the years that it is the little things that are important. It is not an expensive dinner or an expensive gift which matters for any occasion it is the little thoughtful things which mean the most like sitting in the rain in a bus shelter thoroughly enjoying chips and we saw the humour of what we were doing. When the rain went off we went for a walk to find a little church at the edge of the forest which I had read about but when we got there the door was locked with a note saying that the key was at the castle which was nearby. We went to the castle and knocked on the door which was a tiny little door in a big gate at the entrance and a lady came out and gave us the key for us to go the very next day. It was so trusting of her to do this and we appreciated it very much.

We returned to the church the next morning and had time to ourselves inside and it was a charming old church with angels painted all over the ceiling. I have always had a great fondness for tiny little country churches and there are quite a few in North Wales and once again it is the little things which mean so much not a grand cathedral but a tiny little place which has given refuge to many over the centuries.

The little things whether it is a smile to a stranger or a little gift to a friend are the things which matter and every little act of kindness can bring so much cheer to a heart which needs warmth and love. Let us all remember how precious the small things are in life and of how rich we truly are when we look around and see the treasures we have in our lives and the friends who bring us little acts of kindness.

See how many little things you can share to bring the sunshine into the lives of others for they truly are some of life's greatest gifts.

The Golden Chalice

I bring to you a golden chalice made from the flower of a golden crocus. Take this chalice and drink the sweetest nectar from it allowing the gold to move through you and fill you. See that gold go into any part of your physical body which needs healing and see it going into your heart to heal any emotions which you may be dealing with at the moment then let it flow into your aura.

This sacred cup of gold is brought to you for what ever you need at this very moment for the gold can heal like nothing else for it is the golden light the same as the Sun, the golden light of wisdom.

This golden cup initiates you into the realm of the gold and the golden realm is a magnificent sight to behold. Let this golden liquid within the gold chalice transport you into the land of golden light and there you will find the great beings whose faces shine like a thousand suns.

Whenever we work with the gold we are working with pure wisdom and it is wisdom which heals all things. A golden flower or a yellow flower is always a symbol of the soul and so when ever you connect to this flower you are connecting to your very own soul and it is your soul which is the keeper of your wisdom.

Just see what happens after you have received this gift and you will be aware of the golden light shining all around you and you will feel in that light the peace and the beauty of your soul. The voice you hear at times, the silent voice within your mind is the voice of yourself as it guides you through life and shows you where you need to go.

The further along this path you tread the more you will be guided by your very own soul so that you always go the right way. Listen within the gold and you will hear that voice and you will find the comfort from the knowledge that there is a greater light taking care of you.

The golden angels come to you as guardian angels; these higher beings who come to look after us and show us the way are always there and all you have to do is to ask for help. Remember to ask for what you need for all you need to do is to reach into the gold and you will be given access to unlimited love, light and help.

So take this blessed chalice and drink deeply from it and see what a difference it makes to you and when you walk outside in the garden or in the open spaces and you see the golden crocus remember the message which it brings to you. Whenever you see one of these flowers in your mind reach out and take another drink from it.

Whenever you need to be filled up with the grace of the divine become the chalice yourself and see yourself standing with your arms forming a chalice shape and then draw down the heavenly golden light and fill up your own chalice. You can always refill from the everlasting golden light which waits to bring its blessings to you.

The Full Moon

Today is the day of the full moon and when the moon shines its light at its fullness then it shines the light deep into our being, deep into the subconscious world of the emotions. The moon is the water element and it governs our waters, our emotional body and so today you have the perfect opportunity to allow the light to go so deep within you to bring to the surface those things which you need to see, those things which have been pushed down for so long. You pushed them down because you could not deal with them, it was too much but now with this beautiful moonlight bring them up to the surface so that they may be acknowledged, healed and released.

We all have within us a root, the root which was planted at the very beginning when the emotional patterns which have followed us throughout our lives were first conceived. As healers our first responsibility is to ourselves and that is to find this root and heal and by doing this we then gain the wisdom to do the same for those who come to us for help. What I have learned is that even though there is the original root, the original which often stems from childhood there can be another root which came into being at another point in your life and even though the first is always the most important, to create complete healing you need to find this other root and indeed there may be more than one. These are the roots which were planted at times in your life when you may have gone through very difficult occasions emotionally and so they created further patterns within your emotional body.

See yourself sitting beneath the full moon and watch as it beams down its white silvery light creating a circle around you with you in the centre. Take that light in so that you become the moon and shine so brightly then go into your heart and go behind the heart and follow the black tunnel which you will find there down to the very roots of your being. Sit within this black light but at the same time you will still shine with the moon light so you have the light to see.

Allow the memories to come to the surface, memories which you have pushed down for so long, memories of those painful times when you held in all that you were feeling. Feel them again and relive the situations and see the truth completely. We cannot look to anyone else for what they have done to us for they have only been our teachers who provided the teachings of what we have come here to learn.

Feel all the pain you find and your very often it is the pain of what you have allowed and there will be situations where you have had no choice but to allow what ever took place for fear of what may have happened to you. Until we find all the roots within us of our emotional patterns and pain we are never free but when you are to find what is at the bottom of everything and you find not only the original beginning of your wound but also the other wounds which went on top of those at other times in your life you will be free. Whatever you find whether it is guilt, jealousy, resentment, anger, rejection, no matter what it is claim it and allow it like never before and give yourself the fullest permission to accept what you see. Love yourself, love yourself in wholeness and that means accepting your guilt and your rejection and all these other things, love them for they are part of you, they have been your teachers. Feel the pain you have carried for so long and set it free with love. There comes a time on the spiritual journey when you get at last to say yes this is what is at the bottom of everything for me and how I have suffered and how I have disregarded myself and given myself away but now it is time to love it all and claim it all back. Rejoice in your sovereignty when you take back your power once you have found the truth which lies beneath. Take your power from situations and from all those people whom you have given it to. Your sovereignty has been so hard won for you have suffered so much to claim it.

When you open yourself up and see what is within it is the most beautiful thing for the truth lies not in becoming an ascended being filled with shimmering light you are at your most shimmering when you descend, when you descend into the darkness where all your deepest treasures are.

This is spiritual ascension but in truth it is about descending for this is what makes you authentic when you stand in your magnificence with all the emotions you have tried to deny and you love it all and you no longer look to others for what they have done to you. You know without a doubt that there is no need for any entities, curses or anything else to be removed from you which you may have been told by others for it all belongs to you every bit of it. No one can take it away from you for it is yours and it is from the anger and guilt and the rejection that the greatest treasures you will ever find will be given to you.

Love yourself like never before and that love will heal you and when we truly love ourselves we see ourselves in our totality with all our flaws and in all our magnificence and when you do this you will light up the whole universe.

The storms rage here today so see them as a symbol for the raging storms within which we have all pushed down so far into our being and know that it is time now for them to see the light of day and be blown free by the winds of change

Much love to you all on this full moon day and may the lunar light be a lantern to light your way.

Self Care

It is so important on your spiritual journey to
remember self care.

Many of you spend much time helping and healing
others and so you too need time just for you and your
own healing.

There are so many ways of healing your mind and
your body and today the crystal realm is calling out to
you for you to make your connections and use the
crystalline energy to heal and renew yourself. Every
now and again the realm of the crystals reaches out to
us to really connect and today its energy is very
powerful. Whenever crystal energy contacts us it
always brings clarity, it brings clarity for the mind so
that you can understand and heal your emotions and it
brings clarity to the energies of the body so that it can
transform and clear the old stuck energies which are
really old stuck emotions.

Reach out before you and you will find crystals will
manifest in the air around you and they will be just the
ones which you need at this time. Take them and place
them in your chakras or in your organs or put yourself
right inside one and watch as the crystal begins to melt

away and transform all that you no longer need. Use the crystals in their light form for your physical symptoms as well as for your emotional healing and they will bring great relief from pain and stress.

Each crystal has its own properties and it is just the same when working with crystals of light as it is when working with physical crystals and so you can feel into what each one brings for you. Try this today and spend some time just with yourself for your own healing and you will be amazed at how much clearer and how much more energised you will feel.

If you have stomach problems bring in citrine and place it in your stomach and let it melt within and do its work. If you are suffering in the heart then use a ruby or an emerald. If your mind is filled with doubts and confusion then place clear quartz around your head. Sapphire will always bring you deep healing and you can even visualise yourself wearing clothes made of a gem. The ways you can use crystals which you manifest as light are unlimited. You can even visualise making yourself a drink from crystal and sit and feel that crystalline energy move through you as you sip it. If you need nurturing then bring in rose quartz, make it into a cream and rub it into your aura and feel how soothing this is. If you have trouble speaking out and you hold back your words then place aquamarine in your throat and watch as it dissolves there dissolving the old energies which have been held in so that you can then speak with crystal clarity.

When you use crystals in this way very often they will be present within you for about three days and after that time they will have been fully absorbed within your energy field and they will have done their work so keep connected to them for the next few days and see what a difference they make. Open your mind to all the magical ways you can use crystal energy to heal yourself. Visualise a crown of diamonds to clear your thoughts or put on a dress of any gemstone and allow its healing qualities to permeate through every part of you and all your bodies.

Take time for yourself and always remember to do this for you give so much of yourself to others, don't leave yourself out, hear the call of the crystalline realm and let it welcome you into its arms and bring you healing, nurturing and the comfort that you need.

Earth Healing

The natural world is like a medicine chest for it contains unlimited healing plants and we can use these plants as physical remedies or we can manifest them as light. It is good to take plant medicines for they are filled with the life force of mother Earth but it can be even more powerful to manifest remedies of light by visualising the plants and using them for healing.

I have been given three plants for you to bring you healing for what ever you need so open your mind up to the possibility and the belief that you can be healed on many levels.

The first plant for you was brought to me first of all by my father and it is sage. My father was a wonderful man from Cork who shared his love of the land and his knowledge of the healing properties of nature with us all from the time I was a little girl. He was Uncle Tom to my many, many cousins and sometimes I bring Uncle Tom's remedies to share with you and this is one of them. He was also known as Dr. Quack by my family because he always had a remedy for everything. Those were the days when natural medicine was still very much the domain of very few people.

Sage is an incredible healer for it purifies and also the clue is in its name; always look to the names of plants to discover more about them. Sage is wisdom and wisdom is the greatest healer for when we understand why we have problems and we gain wisdom and teachings from them then you are connecting to the inner sage.

Visualise yourself moving sage leaves through your aura from head to toe and watch as any stagnant energies are transformed into new energy. You can use the plants in any way to bring you healing so let the plant spirit speak to you and show you how you can heal yourself.

The second plant brought to you is the wild pink thornless rose from the garden of St Francis in Assisi and it is brought to you by Francis. This rose can heal your mind for it is in our minds where we carry old repetitive thoughts and those things which we hang onto from our past. He explains how these thoughts become like a crown of thorns upon our head and we carry the pain and burden of those things we are hanging onto and the hurt which has been done to us. He asks you to take this pink wild thornless rose and rub it between your hands so that it turns into oil then place this in the aura around your head. By doing this it will transform your old thoughts into new thoughts.

The third plant brought to you is a golden marigold. The marigold is often either brought by Mary Magdalene or mother Mary but this one is given to you from mother Mary. Any golden or yellow flower is a symbol of the soul and when we connect to a golden flower we connect to our very own soul. Take this golden flower from mother Mary and feel how it is filled with the essence of the divine mother and put it within your heart and let its light radiate out through your entire being. Feel the presence of mother Mary as you do this and feel yourself filled with the golden light of your own soul.

This is healing in wholeness for your body, your mind and your spirit and it is brought to you with the greatest love and with the message that you can heal yourself, anything is possible. No matter what you are feeling as you read this, take the hands of mother Mary and Francis for your journey of healing. Turn to the world of plants and use them for your remedies in your daily life and when you sit for the purpose of your own healing or for the healing of others let the plant spirits come to you and work with them and the incredibly transformative powers of the plants whose essence they carry within them.

St. Francis

St Francis is not only associated with animals he is also a new world teacher for the planet. In time to come he will have much to say about the future of the earth as well. He brings knowledge of all the healing gifts of mother Earth, of the plants, trees, herbs and flowers and many other things including the crystals and today he brings the crystal light to you.

Whenever we work with the crystal realms we are connecting to the essence of clarity for crystal energy clears and brings greater awareness. St Francis is a teacher for the heart the same as Christ is and he brings to you a clear quartz crystal in the shape of a heart so if you sit quietly you will feel him place it into that centre.

Crystal energy clears away the old vibrations, it clears your energy field and it brings you the clarity to see what you need to see. Feel Francis put this crystal heart in your heart and then sit with him and you will feel a vibration radiating from his heart into your crystal heart. You will feel it like electricity and the crystal within you will light up and begin to spread through the whole of your body and your energy field clearing away the cobwebs.

Feel anything old within you being transformed into pure crystalline light and feel your heart opening as this takes place. Keep the connection from his heart to your heart and you will be filled with the most divine healing light.

When you have completed this then shine the crystalline light from your heart out into the world and send it to the places which badly need the light. Send the crystal light from your heart to anywhere that you are drawn to. This crystalline vibration which you will send out will be blended with your own heart light with the love which is within you and so the light will be even more powerful than just using the crystal. Using crystalline energy in this way is very, very powerful. Keep connected to the crystal realms of light and bring in crystalline energy for your healing. Visualise a different coloured crystal in each of your chakras or take yourself into a crystal cave; by doing this you will keep your energy strong, vibrant and clear. Use this energy for the Earth and for those around you who need healing.

Let your heart beat with the heartbeat of Francis and may your light shine like a torch clearing and healing all things.

The Sacred Marriage

A few days ago I was standing before my altar
fascinated as I looked at two heart-shaped
candleholders which I have there reflected in the silver
of the chalice behind them. As I looked at the chalice I
could see four candleholders reflected and as I
reflected upon this I heard the words, as above so
below and I was very aware of both the lower self and
the higher self within us all.

Just after that I went and stood beside Graham at the
right side of him where he was working on the
computer and he jumped so much because he said he
had seen me already standing to the left of him. I knew
what he had seen; he had seen another part of me. The
spiritual path is one where the higher self eventually
merges with the lower self and so you have access to
knowledge and ancient wisdom and you have access
to help and guidance whenever you need it. This is all
part of going within to find your answers.

The true guru is the self and the meaning of the word
guru is the one who takes away darkness for when we
step out of the darkness into the light we step into the
full realisation of understanding. Within you you have

your higher self who is always present to nurture you and bring you your answers and all you need to do is to go within and make your connection.

Here are two ways to do this and I'm sure if you use them you will find great comfort and much help and support for you and your life.

Go into your heart and go to the very back of it and there you will see a door and as you step through that door it will be very dark but there will be a tunnel which leads downwards. If you follow that tunnel deep down it will eventually open out and there sitting by a fire in the darkness and in the shadows will be your higher self. She or he will look different to each and every one of you but you will know that they are you and you are them and by your connection with them you can find the help you need.

Another way you can connect to your higher self is that instead of going down the dark tunnel behind the heart if you look up in the same place you will see a golden spiral staircase; if you walk up the staircase it will take you very high and into the most beautiful light. You will eventually arrive at a place filled with light and there your higher self will wait for you dressed in the most beautiful and softest colours and you can sit with them and receive whatever you need to know.

Your inner self, your higher self works constantly to guide you and to lead you in the right direction and it takes practice to trust what you receive but the moment you make this connection the more you will trust and you will find riches beyond measure as you have constant access to wisdom.

So connect to your own guru and let her or him dispel the darkness which are only thoughts and let them bring you into the light of true understanding. This is the sacred marriage where the higher and the lower merge as one.

The Lamp

A long time ago I was given an old-fashioned lamp
from spirit and I was told that I would always have the
light so I would like to share with each and every one
of you a lamp just for you.

Take this lamp and keep it and let it always remind
you that no matter how you feel or what is going on in
your life you always have the light to shine the way
ahead for you. The light is always there even in your
darkest times it is just that you forget about it.

It is so important that every day you bring in that light
and let it shine in all the dark places of your thoughts
and upon those things which are bothering you.

Draw in the light in any way which feels right for you,
I particularly like visualising the sun, drawing in the
sun's radiant light and filling myself with it. This is a
very ancient practice and the ancients knew how
powerful it was.

Take time each day to connect to your light for the
light truly comes from within and it is always there
and you can see it as a little lamp always lit ready to
shine for you.

When we bring the light in for ourselves we also shine more brightly so that others can receive our light and they too will be lit up so that they can see what they need to see.

Your light never goes out it is always there but throughout our busy days and when we fill our mind with worries it can sometimes feel like we are in the dark but this is not so for the light is your birthright, you brought it here with you and it will remain with you for ever more for it is the light of the divine spirit which moves through all things.

No matter what is happening in your life bathe in radiant light and you will immediately feel better in mind and body. Spread the light with your little lamp throughout your home so that its light reaches every corner and each day you will live within that light and you will also shine brighter because of it.

It is the light in others which we are drawn to that is why so many of us will often draw random strangers to us who need a little bit of that light, they feel the light even though they do not know it.

When we are drawn to the warmth of another person it is the light within which pulls us like a magnet and we always feel better for having been in their company so remember the light within and remember your little lamp and take it out if you feel yourself in need of light, bathe within its radiant glow and you will be able to see that everything is just as it is meant to be and all is well.

Hummingbirds

A couple of weeks ago I wrote about how myself and my friend Elaine met for lunch and we couldn't go to the place we had originally decided to go to and we ended up in a third pub and we decided to go inside. That was all meant to be because of the sweet peas I had taken for Elaine which brought communication from the mother of the waitress who served us and who had passed on.

I met Elaine again on Friday and once again the place we had decided to have lunch was not serving food so we tried a second pub and the same thing happened and we ended up in a cafe which we had not intended to go to. Just at the very end of our afternoon Elaine lifted up the lovely china cup that her tea had been served in and there on the cup was a hummingbird.

I wrote last week about my brother passing over and of how the symbol of the hummingbird was his symbol and it is coming up time and time again and here it was again. He has been around me this week and I was able to share this with others and it was such a lovely feeling and I'm sure as time goes on there will be more communications but for now the hummingbird is certainly very much present.

I share this with you to let you know that you really are never alone and that when loved ones pass over they are often still there with you. Look for them in the symbols which you are drawn to.

There is so much revealed to us in the symbolism around us and most of the time we do not take notice of these things but they are all the messages from your loved ones revealing to you that they are there by your side. It is so easy to miss these messages and they can be very subtle but they are there and all it needs is for you to take notice.

You too will find your own symbols of your loved ones and also those in spirit who to come to teach and guide you and you will know that they are present.

Once again Elaine and I had to try three places for lunch but we eventually arrived at the right destination and everything was as it was meant to be.

The Sea

A few days ago I was urged to walk down the lanes to
the sea which is not far from where we live and it was
a beautiful day and I embraced the water element from
the shore. Whenever you are drawn to the sea it is all
about seeing for it brings you a greater ability to see
deeper into things. The water element is so important
in all our healing practices and different types of water
bring different types of healing but the sea brings a
particular vibration. The sea contains salt and nutrients
but more than anything else it helps you to see.
Bring the water into your healing practices for yourself
and for others but when you need to help someone to
see deeper in to their lives or into a situation manifest
seawater for them and use it in whatever way you are
drawn to do.
I walked along the common at the edge of the shore
and in the woods which are set back and I was
absolutely amazed at the variety of wildflowers which
were abundant everywhere. It is a protected area and
many flowers grow here including native orchids but
what I was drawn to more than anything else was
chicory and pink bindweed. These are two unusual

flowers to find growing wild and we do not often come across them but I absolutely love them and I was delighted to find them.

When I arrived back home I was drawn to Google the wildflowers around the Sea of Galilee the place where Mary Magdalene was born and where she spent part of her life and to my surprise chicory and pink bindweed were two of the flowers which were listed. I took myself to the Sea of Galilee which I have done many times before and I spent some time there amongst the flowers and once again it brought me the ability to see more.

If you feel that you need to see more, to understand more about spirit, to understand more about yourself or to understand situations in your life then go to the sea or visualise in your inner journeying the seas within but also take yourself to the Sea of Galilee and spend some time with Mary Magdalene walking along the shore and let her teach you about the wildflowers there, let her take you into the sea and baptise you into new ways as she did many times in her life.

The gift of baptism does not belong with the church for it is an ancient custom to bring you back into the new and you can be baptised time and time again. So go and spend time with Magdalene amongst the flowers for she does indeed bring teachings about the earth

and about the flowers, step into the water and receive her blessed baptism and find yourself renewed.
Then go and sit on the shore with her and fill yourself with the peace of this very special place for it is filled with peace and you will feel it as you sit in the sunshine with the warm breeze surrounding you and the calmness of the waters before you.

The Garden

At the beginning of this year we created our new front garden in what had previously been a small space with an ancient privet hedge and old crazy paving. The hedge was taken out and replaced with wooden fencing and some of the paving stones were taken up to create beds along with the borders.

This was my new rose garden and I planted climbing roses along with jasmine and honeysuckle to grow up the fence and then I planted more roses and lots of other plants as well. I transplanted some seedlings from our back garden and I sowed lots of seeds of my favourite flowers. I have included herbs and marigolds as well which I love.

The climbing roses flowered but they are yet to climb the fence and everything else has been beyond my expectation and the garden has blossomed in such a short space of time. I am used to our back garden which I absolutely love and where I sit to contemplate and it is like woodland surrounded by tall trees but because of the shade in the garden lots of flowers do not bloom as well as they could if they were in the sunshine.

It has been quite a revelation to me to see flowers which would grow moderately in the back garden grow abundantly now in the front garden which is in full sun and it is a good teaching to remind us that we too grow abundantly when we have the light to feed us. Although we need to be in the shade at times when we go within we shine the brightest when we are in full sun for we are just like the plants and when we observe the plant world and the changing seasons we can receive all the wisdom we need to know.

I have plants in my front garden which have been gifts from others and they bring me so much joy and it has been so nice to share these flowers with friends. Last year I wrote about planting my pink dandelion seeds and they flowered beautifully and I saved the seeds and I have grown them again this year in the front garden. They have blossomed and bloomed and formed seedheads just like dandelions do and so now I have seeds for next year and also I have given some away.

The pink dandelions have been very special to me and it has been so joyous to see how abundantly they have created their seeds. I can grow flowers now which never flowered well before in the back garden and for the first time I have a hollyhock in bloom and tall sunflowers ready to form their flowers. The small calendula I would always grow in the back are now abundant and so tall in the front. The roses are repeat flowering ones and they will continue to provide their blooms and each one which has flowered has been very special to me and it has been amazing to see how in such a short space of time a forgotten space can be so abundant.

We are like the flowers we need the light so step out into the light do not remain in the shadows and you will be seen and you will not be afraid to show your true colours and the beauty of your true self.

The Bee With One Wing

About a month ago Graham and I discovered a bee
with one wing in our garden just by where I usually
sit, it was nestled amongst the marjoram flowers and
from that first moment when we saw it we made a
point of always looking out for it. It lived on the
marjoram for about three weeks and each day we
would make sure that it had flowers to feed from and
if we found it on the path Graham would gently put it
back.

The garden is full of marjoram of white and different
shades of pink and these all came from one sprig of the
herb which a friend had given me a long time ago and
which rooted and consequently spread everywhere in
the garden. I am marjoram because I carry part of her
name in my name and a dear friend of mine Jenny
always calls me Marji.

Life is a mirror and everything around us is one huge
mirror reflecting back to us where we are at and so this
beautiful bee with one wing upon the marjoram was
the energy around me and so I knew that at that time I
only had one wing as well. The bee would alternate
between the different marjoram plants and never

strayed far from its new home. Although we were saddened that this beautiful bee only had one wing and couldn't fly we knew that it was nourished each day by the herb.

I work with symbolism in everything that I do for it is the language of light, the language of spirit and it teaches me much each day so as I reflected upon only having one wing for that time I knew it to be true for I was spending a lot of time in deep contemplation and I knew I needed to be still. There are times upon our spiritual journey and in our lives where we need to stop and be grounded and reflect and digest and see where we are going next.

I accepted that time of not being able to fly and it brought me much understanding of myself and the things I was reflecting upon and it was time very well spent. For all of us these times will come and all we need to do is to surrender to them for we cannot move on into another stage of understanding until we have fully digested the things we have learnt about ourselves. There will be times in your life where you feel that you are at a standstill but that is not the truth of it you are just in the space between, reflecting and digesting and it is during that time where inspiration can knock upon the door for inspiration cannot enter until we have first cleared out.

Earlier this week we saw our beautiful bee make its way down the path and it went behind the bins. I had a marjoram plant in a pot so I placed it near there but we never saw the bee again for its time had come and it knew. We were sad to say goodbye to it but happy that it was set free from a life where it was not able to fly but it taught me much about the lives that we live and of how sometimes we cannot fly free but it is in those times where the greatest gold is, the golden light of wisdom.

I am waiting now to find my other wing and I'm quite happy with just one wing at the moment but I know without a doubt that I will be shown through symbolism my new wing which is waiting for me.

The New Wing

Last Sunday I wrote that I had only had one wing for a few weeks and it was a time for me for deep contemplation. I didn't go on my usual walks and I spent a lot of time going deep within. I also wrote that I would wait for the symbol of a new wing to present itself.

A couple of days ago I felt a box on my lap and when I looked it was tied up with a ribbon and inside was my wing but that wasn't sufficient to let me know that my wing had been returned. Later on I had the confirmation for when I looked out of the window there on my statue of the goddess Flora had landed a red Admiral butterfly and it stayed there for a couple of hours. Then I was convinced I had my two wings back together again courtesy of the beautiful butterfly. The butterfly had landed right upon the heart of the statue and it made me realise that when our wings are returned to us after a period of being grounded it is truly the heart which has the wings, they do not belong upon our backs they belong in the heart. When our heart has its wings it is able to lift up and it is only when we lift up in consciousness that we can see with greater clarity.

Today the red admiral butterfly returned to the garden and it was positioned on the wall opposite the statue again for a couple of hours and I knew it had come to tell me to write about this for this butterfly carries great symbolism. It not only brings us the gift of flight and the essence of transformation but it is the butterfly for the heart for the admiral of the fleet is Christ. When I speak of Christ I am talking about what he symbolises which is always the heart.

When we speak of great beings it doesn't always mean that they actually come to visit us or bring us their messages more often than not it is the idea of them, their essence and what they represent and Christ is the healer and the opener of the heart.

I remember something similar happened some years ago when I was out walking and I just stopped in the middle of some wildflowers and a red admiral butterfly landed on my heart and it stayed there for about 20 minutes. We are indeed blessed when the butterfly alights upon us.

No matter where you are at in your spiritual journey there will always be times when you are grounded so that you can digest and review and go deep within, it is part of the path and it is a very precious time when you come to it.

So go with the flow and if you feel that nothing is happening in your life just know that you are in between stages with one foot in the past and one foot in the future and maybe it is time for you to fold your wings and go deep within and enjoy the revelations which the silence brings to you. Then you too can wait for the symbol of your new wings to be brought to you at the right time.

Gold

A couple of days ago the gold colour came in and its vibration is becoming stronger each day. We are constantly working our way through the rainbow as we receive many colours of light to bring us healing and awakening. Sometimes those colours come in gradually and sometimes they come in very dramatically and we really feel them.

If you take notice of everything around you you will be able to discern which colours you are receiving on a daily basis, look at the colours you are drawn to wear or the colours of the flowers you bring into your home or the colours you notice in your environment and they will all be clues to tell you what is being brought to you.

The golden colour is the ultimate healer for it is the colour of wisdom and it is wisdom which heals us more than anything else. The gold is pouring in and all you need to do is to be aware of it and to let it into your being and it will bring you healing for your physical body and your emotional body too.

Visualise the gold pouring down in through your crown and watch the golden light move like a river through you and let it go to those parts of your body where you have discomfort and let the golden light seep deep into you. Feel it circulate through every part of you down to your toes then watch as it spreads out into your aura so that you are immersed in the gold within and without.

There is gold in abundance around us each day, there is the gold of the sun and the gold from the flowers of the Earth and at this time especially there are many fields of gold where the crops are being harvested for it indeed is a golden time.

Visualise yourself taking in the sunlight and you can do this at any time of day or night, visualise yourself standing upon the earth and take in all the gold colours from all of nature. If you are drawn to a gold or a yellow flower when you are outside or in the garden then let its colour fill you up for even just by standing next to a flower you absorb its light and its colour.

Even these words I am writing for you come on the vibration of gold and so when you read them you will take in the golden colour from the words themselves for behind every written word there is an energy, a vibration which touches you more than the words themselves.

Bathe in the golden light for it is being brought to you and it is at its height today on the day of the full moon and it brings the most perfect balance of lunar and solar energies within you. Use the gold as a tonic at any time and always remember that if you are feeling low or not well then let it bring you its wisdom.

There are many I find at the moment who are suffering from anxiety and depression and finding life very challenging, it seems to be here amongst many people so if you are feeling like this fill yourself with the gold and watch as you feel lighter each time you do this and let the golden light build up within you and you will be given the understanding of those things which are troubling you. It is through the golden light of understanding where you will find your answers and from there you will be able to make peace with yourself and with everything else.

Balance

Yesterday morning as I was looking up at the sky I saw the moon as well as the sun and so I reached up and I drew down the moon and I drew down the sun and I brought both of these beautiful energies into me. I filled up with them and they flowed into my aura. When you work with the moon and the sun together you bring in balance and harmony and they also create the most wonderful light golden coloured light.
No matter what you are healing within yourself whether it is physically or emotionally it is always about balance and so to create balance within just keep bringing yourself back into the centre and into harmony and bring in the sun and the moon together. The solar and lunar energies together bring the most amazing combination of the divine feminine and the divine masculine and so to blend them as one creates the perfect vibration within. Any physical symptoms come from the mind when the mind is dealing with painful memories or painful situations and it is at those times when we are not in harmony and it is meant to be that way. We have to be fully immersed in all our emotional pain and discord to fully heal it.

So feel everything and you will know when you are healed when the old thoughts do not rise again within you or they are not triggered by the actions of another person but for as long as those old thoughts come back into your focus whatever it is you are dealing with has not been healed. So enter into the well of yourself and revisit once again those things which are the roots of any pain you may be feeling emotionally or physically and after you have done this and emptied out fill up with the moon and the sun.

Whenever you empty out it creates an empty space within you and it needs to be filled again with the light and this is a very harmonising way of doing this. There is magic everywhere, there is healing everywhere, mother nature and father sky provide us with so many healing tools and all we need to do is to believe and to reach out and draw in whatever we are drawn to. Your attention will always lead you to what you need. There doesn't have to be a moon visible in the sky at the same time as the sun for we can create all our healing by just going within and manifesting whatever we need. Manifesting anything from the light is even more powerful than using physical things.

Visualise yourself outside on a beautiful sunny day and look up and see the sun and the moon in the sky before you then reach out your arms and draw each one down in turn and let the light combine within you so that you are filled with the most glorious brilliant pale golden light. Let it circulate throughout your body.

If you have pain in any part of you take that combined light and visualise it upon the pain and see it transforming and healing it. If you are suffering from emotional pain then let the light condense in your heart. When you have filled up with the sun and the moon then let this light fill your chakras then radiate out into your aura so that you are lit up like the sun and the moon.

In this way you actually become the sun and the moon and you will radiate such amazing light and that light will shine outwards upon who ever needs harmony and balance within their lives.

The Cave

There are times when we are in the cave and it is during those times where we dive deep within for healing and awakening but there comes a time to step out of the cave.

If you have been experiencing much healing lately and you have felt the need to stand back from the world a little bit to retire in to the quiet within then now is the time to come out of the cave once more.

Our journey is always in cycles just like the seasons and we enter winter but the spring will always come and when it does we step out of the dark and into the light again.

I was shown the scene from when Jesus came out of the cave and Mary Magdalene was waiting for him, remember when we work with spirit everything is symbolic with greater meaning for us to understand. Jesus did not die on the cross he was healed and he was helped by his companions with herbs and remedies but we can take the symbolism of this of the resurrection of the self for those times where we need to die to the old and be born again in the new ready for greater awareness and deeper wisdom.

Magdalene was the first to see him and I was shown the two of them today together in the garden. They were married and they had children so their relationship was earthly as well as spiritual and Mary Magdalene carried the ancient mysteries within her the same as Jesus.

As I watched the scene before me I was part of it and Jesus put his hands upon my head and I felt the healing and after this Magdalene held me close heart to heart where our two hearts were touching. I share this with you so that you can experience this wonderful healing for yourself so no matter where you are in your journey it is now time to step out of the cave once more and into the light and rise up in consciousness once more.

Go into the garden and meet Magdalene and Jesus, the perfect balance of male and female, of yin and yang and receive the touch of the hands of Jesus as he places them upon your head and feel the healing fill you so deeply. Then step into the embrace of Magdalene so that your heart rests upon her heart and the healing love will flow from her to you and you will feel held and nourished and nurtured with the most wonderful feeling that all is well.

There is so much healing available to you at this time so allow your own visions to come to you so that you too may receive healing in many ways but for today step out of the cave and into the light and receive these twin gifts of healing. You will find that not only will you receive healing but you will also receive the harmony of the blending of the male and the female life force within you.

May you be healed of all those things which you pray to be healed and may the healing energy flow through you all. Sending much love and healing to each and every one of you.

The Divine Masculine

Although for most of us we work with the divine
feminine at this very moment the divine masculine is
more apparent than ever and we need to connect to it
to bring in the perfect balance. Some of you may have
already felt this as you have been more aware of male
guides around you helping you.

Recently I was in the garden and I was so aware of the
presence of Merlin. Even though the actual Merlin is
far removed from the mystical Merlin whom we know
and love I felt Merlin as the most amazing cosmic
being and he overlaid me and I felt him in physical
form. When we work with Merlin we are working with
the essence of magic and all magic is is transformation
and in our work as healers we are transformers
transforming old energies into new.

As he overlaid me I felt how tall he was and he was
very well made with large hands, he had a long white
beard and the most piercing eyes. I knew that I had to
go from the garden outside to the trees beyond and I
was so drawn to the hazel tree and if I could have
found a branch on the ground I would have taken one
for a wand. After this he placed in my hands a book

and a candle and he asked me to go inside and pick a card from my mists of Avalon oracle deck and he said the card I would choose would be the Merlin one.

I came in and shuffled the cards and just as he said the card I chose was Merlin and amongst the other things before him in the picture was a candle and a book but what surprised me more than anything was that in his left hand he was holding an emerald fire.

The previous week I had noticed an emerald fire amongst the trees in my little wooded area at the bottom of the garden then I saw emeralds sitting on the leaves of other trees. I went deep within and a male being of light came to me and took me deep into the earth where he picked up a lantern of emerald fire and then he gathered emeralds and as I followed him he brought those emeralds to the surface of the Earth. I was asked to work with the emerald fire to create an emerald temple in the etheric realms.

After this I organised an evening with the priestesses and high priestesses whom I teach and we worked with the emerald fire within an emerald temple and the energy from all of this felt so powerful and so ancient and so healing.

It was only when Merlin came to me in the garden that I realised he was the being of light who had taken me deep into the earth to retrieve the emerald fire and the emeralds.

I was aware of the presence of Merlin following all of this but there was one more connection for me to make. Graham and I have just been to Dorset and to Glastonbury and on our way there we stopped at a service station on the M5 and as soon as we parked a van came and parked right next to us and on the side of it was written Merlin Van Hire with a picture of Merlin. This was to remind me of his presence so that I would keep my connection to him.

I give to each of you the emerald fire which Merlin brought and you can use it to heal yourself in any way that you are drawn to. Put it on any pain you have, put it in your heart or just sit within it and you will feel the magic of the transformation which this brings to you. Magic is all around at this time and it comes to you with its true meaning of transformation and every time we let go and heal a little bit more we create the deepest magic.

May the emerald fire and the magic of Merlin surround you all your days and remember one more thing, magic is belief so believe in yourself and the unlimited healing which is always there for you.

The Bridesmaid

My sister recently found a photograph and sent it to me and it was taken 50 years ago when I was a bridesmaid at her wedding. A lot of water has gone under the bridge since then and as I looked back and reflected I learned much about myself.

It was the following year after this when something traumatic happened to me and then I found myself drawing many people into my life who were controlling and so I lost my voice. I was always a quiet person from childhood but this was different and from that time I held in much. It never prevented me from enjoying life and having many adventures and good friends who saved me time and time again but I was never completely myself.

We draw situations and people to us as teachers for they teach us where to look and what we need to learn and for me my wound was about rejection and fear of the anger of other people and that fear caused me not to speak out. We bring these wounds with us into this life but it is not past lives where we need to go to retrieve them it is in this current life.

I often look back and I see how much damage I have done to myself by holding in, holding in my feelings and not admitting them and holding in my words all out of fear. I cannot blame those people who controlled me for we can never blame anyone else we always have to look to ourselves for what we have allowed. Ultimately these people bring us blessings for without them we would not be able to heal and learn our lessons.

The years went on and even though I was always outgoing and involved in many things and created many things I would not speak up and I held in my voice. How much damage I have done to myself and how much damage I needed to undo.

The door opened to healing when I first really spoke out and gave someone my truth and it was a shock to me because it came out with such force for so much had been held in for so long. I then began to speak out and to feel my feelings and this took much practice until eventually so much was healed and I do not hold in anything any more.

Whenever we hold in our feelings we do not allow ourselves to see the full truth of people and things and the energy of these feelings stays within the energy body and consequently the physical body. Everything we hold in stays within and I held in so very much over the years. I have healed from this but the truth is the healing never stops and we still get tested at times to make sure that we have learned our lessons.

So my reflections from 50 years ago have given me an even deeper understanding of the healing process within me and I share this with you to say to you never hold anything in, let it out, don't make excuses for other people, allow yourself to see the truth and then speak your truth. Never look to anyone else for what they have done to you for you have allowed everything. Where ever you are in your own healing journey and for most people this centres around being totally yourself and being true to yourself and speaking your truth; remember that if you hold in your feelings they will stay within you so set yourself free and just be yourself completely.

I look back and see all the damage I have done to myself, I have done it but without it I would not have learnt my lessons; what a great blessing this is for we come to this earth to come to school to learn until eventually we understand that we are magnificent beings of love and light.

We come to love ourselves by being ourselves and that is the ultimate healing.

Connections

After bumping into an old friend yesterday at the beach I reflected upon how we are always in the right place at the right time.

Although I am from the north-east of England I came to teacher training college in Liverpool and it was there where I met my first husband and we went back to my hometown to live.

Little did I know I was meant to return back to the area where we live now which is on the Wirral across the River Mersey from Liverpool.

After spending 11 years teaching in my place of birth Alan was offered a job looking after the homeless running the night shelter beneath Liverpool Metropolitan Cathedral and so we came back.

After my divorce from Alan I met Graham but I was always intrigued as to why Graham and I had never met before this. We had mutual friends and as I had a health food shop I was supposed to give a talk at the local vegetarian group which Graham attended. I cannot remember why that never happened but it obviously wasn't time to meet up with him.

Eventually Graham and I married and settled in Moreton and it just so happened that the lady who was my spiritual teacher lived in Moreton also and for the next 17 years I was a constant visitor at her house receiving teachings.

That was no coincidence.

I can walk easily to the sea from our house and as I reflected upon meeting an old friend yesterday I knew once again how important it is for me to be by water. I grew up by the sea and I spent a good part of my youth on the beach with many happy memories.

Some time before I met Graham I had a reading from a lady who used to set an alarm clock so that you didn't go one minute over time. I love the old mediums and their quirky ways.

She told me that Moreton would be very important to me in the future and I had no idea why, it was never a place I would have considered living in but it came to be.

Looking back on all of this I realised more than ever what I already know that we are always in the right place at the right time.

I share this with you so that whatever you are going through in your life or whatever difficulties you are having regarding home, relationships, jobs, anything at all you are always in the right place at the right time.

We cannot be in the right place before time and everything is always on time and we are always where we are meant to be.

So where ever you are just know that everything is as it is meant to be and take comfort in the knowledge that you are always guided by unseen forces to be in the right place at the right time.

Guardian Angels

A few days ago I was pondering about something and looking for an answer and I couldn't find one then suddenly I was very aware of a golden angel surrounding me. I am not one for Angels but I recognised this one for it was my own guardian angel. Your guardian angel is your own true higher self the one who holds you throughout your life looking after you and guiding you in the right direction. People see angels with wings but that is only symbolic and even though I don't particularly connect to Angels myself I know angelic energy when it comes around me. It is light and lightness itself.

My golden angel held me and I felt the most beautiful golden feathers as I have seen them before, remember this is all symbolic language for our human minds can only understand things through what we know.

I was lifted up through realms of light until I was eventually brought to a place of even greater light. As I rested in that light the answer to my question was given to me.

I realised then that I had forgotten something that when we are looking for the answer to something we will not find it where we are with our rational minds for we need to lift up so that we can see with clarity. If you are looking for answers to your questions then you need to lift up too.

You can lift up in any way that you choose, you can visualise a golden angel lifting you up to the higher realms of light or you could take yourself to the top of a mountain.

The mountains are always a symbol of the higher self but whichever way you rise up to higher ground just know that it is there where you will find what you are looking for. You need to lift up so that the mind lifts up and receives greater vision. We cannot discover understanding when we are too close to things we need the distance for the greater clarity which comes from seeing things from a higher perspective.

Fly high on your own or with your angels, climb the highest mountains, go to the Himalayas or even ascend up into the night sky and see the earth below you then sit within the energy and ask your question and the answer will come to you.

Our journey is the journey into higher consciousness and we can use the symbolism of rising higher this is why enlightenment is now called ascension but all it means is rising into the light to see things clearly.

Maybe your own golden guardian angel will come to you and hold you close and you too will see the details of the golden feathers and you will feel the love which will come from your angel. You will feel held like nothing else can hold you and you will feel safe in the knowledge that where ever you go there is always an angel walking by your side and that angel is your own divine soul.

Colours

It is fabulous that there is a vegan chef on the Bake off on television and she did well last week showing that vegan baking can be as delicious and attractive as any other type of baking.

I was reading an article about Prue Leith, a presenter on the Bake Off who was advocating that older women wear bright clothes. She wears the brightest clothes of all different colours and she looks amazing.

The colours we choose to wear are very important for we absorb the colours from our food, from our clothing and from our surroundings without us realising it and often instinctively we choose the colours we need.

Sometimes people do not wear bright colours for fear of being seen and they feel that they can remain more hidden if they wear neutral or dark colours. When you wear bright colours you bring in brightness and you radiate brightness.

Many people like to wear much black and it is a wonderful colour to wear but it is important that we change our colours often rather than stay in one energy continuously.

Black is the colour of the deepest wisdom and Mary Magdalene brings the black as a black robed Nazarene priestess and the witch is epitomised in black. This is all because black enables you to access the deepest ancient mysteries.

Wear black if it feels right for you but also wear the rainbow and work your way through the rainbow and see how you feel. Colour heals us and even through our food it is the colour spiritually which brings us healing.

Let yourself be seen through the bright colours you wear and become the rainbow not afraid to show your true colours then radiate your rainbow light to touch those who remain in the shadows.

Coincidences

On Friday I caught a bus to meet my friend Elaine for
lunch and an old medium friend of mine was also on
the same bus. As we chatted he told me that my old
teacher who has passed was around me and I am sure
that she had a hand in what was to transpire.
As we were talking I remembered that some time ago
Elaine had asked me to get his phone number if I met
him again so that she could have a reading from him.
Neither of us had a pen and so he suggested that he
would get off the bus with me and come to the pub for
a drink and he could arrange something with her then.
So we all sat in the pub having our drinks and then he
decided to have lunch with us. I knew that my old
teacher Romely did have a hand in this for he had
missed his bus and he shouldn't have been on the one I
was on and also I knew that he had received the
feeling that he needed to stay and spend time with us.
So Elaine arranged a time for her reading and we
enjoyed our lunch but as soon as we finished he began
to pick things up for me and he gave me quite a
reading. He picked up all my family members with
their names and all about them and he reminded me

very much of when sometimes Romely would spend an afternoon going through my whole family in the same way. She would often sort everyone out in one go.

So we spent our afternoon in the pub with my old friend in full flow and I was very fortunate to receive so much. He even picked up my brother who has recently passed.

The last time I had a reading from him was about 25 years ago and what he told me then was so right and came to be but I never expected this on Friday afternoon. Spirit always organise things for us, they organise everything and especially if we listen and go with what we feel. If they want us to be in a certain place at a certain time then it will be so.

There are times for all of us especially when we go through challenges where we feel there is no one around us and even though we trust and know in one sense that we are always looked after and that there are always those in spirit around us sometimes we just cannot feel it.

When he described how many I had around me it brought it back home to me how much we are all loved and how much we are held in love from those in spirit. It was so reassuring to hear this.

Just know that you are never alone, there is always someone holding you and directing you and holding you in their love and no matter how much at times you may feel on your own believe me you never are. We are held always by spirit and they will always make sure as well as I have mentioned before that everything is on time and we are always in the right place at the right time.

Ancient Healing Methods

The ancients knew the secrets of sacred geometry and they also had access to many healing techniques which were passed down through the generations and we can still have access to those ways of healing now in the present and I would like to share a few of these with you.

The first one is palming and although this is one of the primary principles of the Bates Method for improving eyesight it is actually an old Tibetan healing method. It really is an incredible healing to use for anything for it creates deep relaxation.

You rub the palms of your hands together and then you cross them covering your eyes blocking out all light. You can manifest a beautiful scene before you or go into a visualisation or meditation and you will find yourself falling into deep calmness. The centres of the palms of your hands have chakras in them and so not only are you receiving the benefit of blocking out the light so that you can relax you are also channelling healing energy through you and in to you.

The second healing I will share with you is the Tibetan figure of eight. I was taught this many years ago when

I practiced kinesiology and I have used it ever since. The figure of eight is also the infinity sign when it is placed on its side and so it encompasses the whole essence of creation and the infinite light held within. Shapes have power the same as words and we can use them to place within the body or even to place within the earth to create healing. With the figure of eight what you do is to trace it three times with your finger over the body or over an area where there is pain or discomfort. I have always begun doing this clockwise. So draw it to cover the body or just draw it over anywhere on the body which needs healing even upon a fairly small place. You draw the symbol and you allow the energy to be absorbed within the energy field and you sit within the energy and let it do its work. The third healing is the five pointed star and again this is a very ancient symbol which has been used for many things but also for healing. Whatever you put inside a five pointed star enhances its vibrations. So if you meditated or performed healing within a five pointed star you would increase the potency of what ever you were doing.

The five pointed star is the star of the elements and I always use the elements of the east and so this star includes the whole cycle of the elements and if you use it for healing you are drawing in the energy of elemental balance and harmony. You can use this star for healing by visualising it or once again tracing it upon any part of the body where healing is needed. These very simple ancient techniques are very powerful for often the simplest things carry the greatest potency. So palm your eyes, use the figure of eight and the five pointed star to create healing and expansion for yourself and see what magic you can create.

Soul Connections

Have you ever met a person and straightaway you have felt a connection with them or have you ever looked into someone else's eyes and seen their soul? We meet people whom we have known in other lifetimes and we feel and sense a connection to them and then there are those people where we can look beyond the veil and see them as they truly are.

We all have our own personal ideas of what the soul is like and this can be anything from a golden guardian angel, a being of white pearl or a Diamond light body but we can only interpret what we see through our limited earthly understanding. It is the feelings which will speak to you and to what you are seeing.

Last week when I was working with a client I saw her soul, remember that what ever we see it is symbolic for symbolism is the language of light, the language of spirit and it is through interpreting what we see that we can fully understand what we are being shown. What I saw was the most beautiful thing. I was taken into a golden cave where it was completely made of the most brilliant radiant gold and in the centre of the cave was a huge diamond and as the light from the gold touched the diamond centre rainbows of light filled the cave. I felt this within me but it wasn't for me it was for the person whom I was working with and I described what I was seeing to her. She then experienced it for herself.

I also saw these rainbows of light move through her and out of her mouth and radiate outwards and I could see them covering a room full of people when she was teaching. The students received the rainbows which were coming from her soul, they were held in that light and they were healed in that light and they were awakened in that light.

No matter how much we learn and know about the spiritual realms the truth is we know nothing and whatever we do know is only a fraction of the truth but when we sense we know and we see the truth and the beauty I saw that day as I saw into that lady's soul stayed with me and revealed to me once more the vastness of the soul.

When you are with people you may get glimpses too and it is often just a fleeting glimpse of the beauty which they carry within and it is the most beautiful connection you can ever make with another person. It is our souls who recognise each other as we journey through life and it is our souls who touch others when we connect to them. It is the soul light which is infinite love which touches people.

It is good to spend time with others to laugh and to share and to sometimes have a good moan but it is the light that we share between us which affects us more than anything else and when you sit in the company of another beautiful soul their light radiates out to you and holds you in its love.

My Broomstick

The other day I had the feeling to go and get my broomstick which was amongst the trees at the bottom of the garden and I leaned it against a table which I could see from the kitchen window. The next day when I looked out of the window it had stood up on its own and it was standing there away from the table. I knew that it was trying to get my attention.

A broomstick can mean many things, it can mean that it is time to sweep away the old to make room for the new, it can mean that it's time to go flying which means inner journeying into other realms but I knew what this meant and I had been feeling it for days. It was the call of the witch within and as we approach Samhain the energies of the witch or the old crone are making themselves known.

Although we apply the term witch to female energies it is the same as the magician within the male and both of these are extremely powerful vibrations. Sometimes when we feel the call of the witch it is to connect us to our inner witch but there are times where we actually have a guide who wishes to make themself known as well.

The energy of the witch brings you freedom for not only does she have command of the elements and she knows the secret of magic which is just transformation she is also a free spirit and that is her essence. When she comes calling she brings to you the ability to be truly yourself and to find the freedom which this brings. Whether we work with these archetypes or actual guides we are bringing to us such a powerful energy and it is in that energy where you can be free to be yourself. She doesn't care what people think, she can laugh and cackle, she can call up the wind or make magic and bring in her healing remedies but she is totally comfortable in her own presence.

Call upon her and transform yourself into her or into him if you are male, into the magician within and throw your arms up in the air and declare your freedom. Draw in the elements and the elementals, bring the herbs into your daily life for healing and for cooking and go into the light and make potions from the plant world and you will find that these are more powerful than physical remedies.

Laugh to your heart's content, wear black if you are drawn to do so for black takes us into the deepest wisdom of ourselves and it brings up the ancient mysteries stored within us.

Samhain is the time of letting go for it is about endings and new beginnings and a week today it will be New Year's Eve in the yearly cycle so let go as much as you can this week in preparation for moving through the gateway from the past and into the future and accept your witch or magician self. Let them become part of you so that you always have a connection to the freedom within and the great unlimited magic with its power of transformation to call upon at any time.

The Heart

This is very much a heart time for the physical heart and for the emotional heart. Many of you are delving deep within to discover even more healing and everything we do to heal ourselves all centres around the heart, everything centres around the heart.

The reason you have suffered both physically and emotionally is because you have not always fully followed your heart. Our heart is our inner compass and it lets us know which way to go and it shows us what it is that we truly desire in life. The problem is that we are often not able to follow our hearts because of circumstances or because we are not ready to reveal our true selves to the world.

When we follow our hearts we are following the call of the soul as it leads us to where we wish to go but at the same time everything in your life and in your past has always been and always is perfect, perfect for your journey for what you need to learn.

There are so many expressions around the heart, heartfelt, broken hearted, whole heartedness, your heart drops, heartless and so many more. Where you are at now in accessing the deepest parts of yourself and the deepest healing just for you is in your heart and the more you can follow the urgings of it the more healing you will receive.

There are many times in my life when I look back where I have not followed my heart to please people because I did not want to upset them but I knew that my heart always knew where I really needed to be. I have learned valuable lessons from all of this and so are you too but it is time now for the healing is ripe and ready for everyone and I know many of you are feeling it. I know many of you are going so deep within to retrieve yourselves and I know also you are feeling the call to retreat away from the world for a little while.

We often all feel things on a universal level and by this I do not mean that we are picking up universal energies and it is those energies which create problems for us, that is not the case for all our feelings belong to us, what I do mean is that many people go through the same things at the same time and this is what is happening right now as we all move deeper into our heart space.

You may hear of people with heart problems for their hearts are ready to awaken and to heal further but all our hearts are ready to burst open like never before. We have help for this, helpers from the realms of light who are there supporting us and holding us at this time of great healing and awakening. The great ones in spirit bring their essence but in truth it is not they who come around you it is the energy they represent and this is the same with gods and goddesses and we can call upon those energies to help us to understand and to heal.

We know about the light of St Francis and his connection to helping the animals and also his connection in the creating of the new earth. There is a saying accredited to him about acceptance but that did not come from him it came from someone else. What he does bring is the knowledge of the heart and the acceptance of following the heart.

We are all in this together, we are all going through the same processes in our own ways opening and opening so that every corner within is cleared and all of this leads us to the heart.

It is our hearts which connect us and it is the love within them which links us all together and it is that love which heals and the more we access what is truly in our heart the more we can all heal for we will be following our true path which is the path to the real and true and authentic self who is totally unmasked.

Renewal

I found the most surprising thing the other day in one of my flower pots in the garden where a yellow daisy had died and a new flower had sprouted from the centre of the blossom. I have only ever seen this before in marigolds and it is something which can happen but what a wonderful teaching it brings.

The old flower died away but from it sprung a new flower and what a wonderful metaphor this is for not only reincarnation but also for our daily renewal for we can renew ourselves every moment of every day and move from the old self into the new self.

What I found interesting as well is that in Chinese philosophy the yellow flower or the golden flower is a symbol for the soul and I know that whenever I work with a yellow flower or I am drawn to one that it is soul work.

Many of you have practised healing modalities like reflexology and working with energies and the knowledge of this has come from the east and from the understanding of the five elements. This is the basis of all Oriental teachings and Oriental healing. The ancient ones there were so in tune with the landscape and the elements and through their observation they learned the secrets of energy flows and they applied that knowledge to the human body. Everything is a mirror for everything else.

By observing the changing seasons and the workings of the elements they gained such a great understanding of the health of the body and because of that they understood how to bring harmony and healing back into the physical self.

So I bring to each of you a yellow flower, a symbol of the origin of much of the healing ways which we know about and practice and also a symbol of the soul. We are moving into a time where everything that we do will be done soul to soul and all the healing work we carry out will come from a very deep place within.

We come back again and again and reincarnate and we continue the work we have done in other lives and we continue the lessons which we have brought back with us to bring them to completion. We pick up where we left off and we come back with our own soul family so that everyone in your life at this moment has already been with you before. This is why we can often feel such a deep connection with a person when we first meet them.

The yellow flower growing from the old yellow flower in my garden showed me so much and reminded me of our journey here and of how we are always letting go and shedding a skin and moving on and each time we are renewed. This is the process of regeneration as we make the journey back to harmony and back to the true self.

Nature has always been my greatest teacher and it remains so and we can be like the ancients making our observations and learning the secrets which mother earth holds within her heart to share with us.

Take this yellow flower I give to you and take it as a symbol of renewal and of how each day contains the unlimited possibilities for new beginnings.

We are all connected soul to soul and we all touch one another with our light and that light is constantly being renewed.

The Woods

Yesterday I spent the afternoon in the woods with a friend and we were that deep in conversation we didn't realise that it had started to get dark and so we decided to make a move. By the time we came out of the woods it was very dark and also we hadn't realised that it had been raining as well.

I have no fear of being in the woods in the dark and there is such a lovely feeling, totally different from the daytime particularly when the moon has just been full. Although I love to go roaming and I have often been quite reckless in the past in walking on the moors or in the hills when it is dark I never had any fear. I would not do that now for there is a time to be sensible and when I look back and see how carefree I have been it made me look at fear.

Even though I have fear in me in the form of phobias and they can be overwhelming at times I would have no fear of being out on my own in dark places. There have been other things in my life which I have dealt with and had no fear but yet to this day I still have my own form of fear and anxiety within.

After being in the woods yesterday in the dark I reflected upon how we all have our own fears but in different ways but fear is fear and it doesn't matter what your fear is even if it is about material things, it doesn't matter it is all fear. Sometimes people think that they are the only ones who feel fear as they do but let me reassure you they are not. A friend went to a well-being class this last week as she suffers from anxiety and it really helped her to be with other people to see that there were many others who felt that way. So no matter what your fear is never have any shame over it or feel that you shouldn't be like that, fear is your teacher and sometimes it is the only thing which will turn us to look inwards. We are all different so embrace your fear and love it and know that it makes you who you are for it helps you to have more empathy with others. If someone has never really experienced deep fear they can never understand how it can rule your life and maybe their viewpoint would be to just get on with it. That is not the answer for it is showing us where we need to look and what we need to heal and it is meant to be.

As a very young child I would scramble down the high cliffs in my home town to pick the pink sea thrift flowers for any flowers were a magnet for me and I would have to pick them. It is quite strange that I don't like heights now and my legs will go wobbly in high places. We are all unique and we are all different and yet underneath the truth is we are all the same.

We all have anxieties and some of them can be covered up very well and no one would know and in my experience you can only share these things with someone who will not judge you and someone who can understand. Sometimes sharing your fears and anxieties can make it worse if it is not the right person but if you are like me and you can be overwhelmed then just know how precious this is for it enables us to truly understand others without any judgement.

So where ever you whether you have personal fears or you are fearful about the events in the world just know that you are not alone and that it is your deep sensitivity to everything which makes you feel so very much.

We Are The Colours

Whenever I cook for guests I always instinctively choose foods which will bring healing. I do this without thinking about it and then afterwards I understand that the colours and even the choice of cuisine were all just right for what people need.
The colours in our food bring us healing but also the choice of food contributes to that healing, root vegetables will heal the roots of your emotions, salad brings lightness, slow cooked foods bring in the fire element and deserts bring the sweetness of life. The type of food and where it has originated from also adds to the vibrations of what you provide, for example Mexican and Indian food bring sunshine and the spice of life.
I have been aware of what I have been doing for a very long time but I also have had further insight into this recently. I realise that the colours that we wear bring healing to those whose company we are in. Without realising it we choose which colours to wear each day and they are the colours we are working with at that time but also we radiate those colours out to others for their healing when we meet them.

Whatever colours we are wearing they are the vibrations we need and what we are working with but you also give those colours out. If you are working with the fire you might choose red, if you feel a greater sense of love then you will choose pink and each colour brings its own particular quality.

We are walking rainbows for we carry the rainbow of colours within.

Even if physically you do not feel the best your colours can still shine so brightly for they are the colours of your spirit body which is not the same as your physical body. We carry the rainbow where ever we go and we share our rainbow colours to others to lift them up and to bring them healing.

Recently I wanted to wear a top with pink roses on it and I also wanted to give a gift of Turkish delight which is made from rosewater and so I knew that the people I was meeting would benefit from the healing of the rose and indeed their hearts did need some comfort.

I always give flowers to people when I visit them and I bring the colours to them through the flowers but now I know that they also receive the colours they need through the clothes I'm wearing. To understand this brings us a much greater awareness of how we share our light with one another and we share that light to heal, to comfort and to help others.

Sometimes your colours dim when you are down or going through healing but your colours change constantly.

Colours come from our energy body from our rainbow light body and they are always present within us so remember that even if physically you do not feel the best you are still lit up like the rainbow and you shine your rainbow lights upon everyone you come into contact with. You are the colours; you are the rainbow and where ever you go you shine your light so remember when you choose your colours to wear for the day they are not just for you they are for the benefit of everyone you connect to.

The Snowdrop

Recently an old friend of mine who had passed over was with me in the garden and she was pointing things out to me to draw my attention to them so that I would receive information from them. I was very drawn to go to one particular place and there I found the first snowdrop flowering.

Our back garden is filled with snowdrops, they were here when we came and they are a glorious sight when they arrive in flower. Each year I wait for the first ones and I always used to pick them and give them to this particular friend, I did this every year for her.

I looked down in amazement to find this snowdrop in flower on the first day of the year and as always it never ceases to amaze me the magic, the beauty and the tenacity of nature.

The snowdrop is the ultimate symbol of hope for it blooms through the frosts and the snow and reveals so much beauty despite harsh winter conditions. It is the most wonderful symbol of the human spirit of all that we endure and of how we still can bloom and blossom even in our own inner winter time.

Whenever someone in spirit comes to you they come to bring you comfort but also to bring you guidance and in my own experience they will often bring me wisdom by the things I am drawn to and very often this will be out in nature or in the garden. It was with the greatest joy that I discovered this first snowdrop and especially because it meant so much to the person in spirit who was revealing this to me. I might not have seen it if I hadn't been directed to find it as it was tucked away.

The snowdrop is seen as a flower of Mary and the word Mary means healer and so the snowdrop can bring great healing. Flowers are incredible healers for their vibration is a very fine and you do not have to make an essence to receive their healing and you do not even have to go outside and stand beside one all you need to do is to go within and think of the flower, even the name of the flower will connect you to their energy.

If you would like some hope, some resilience and strength think of the snowdrop and you will immediately be filled with its healing qualities and you too will bloom and blossom even when the days are cold.

Nature has consciousness and there is nothing which does not have consciousness and nature provides us with many healing gifts and all you need to do is to make a connection and you will be filled with healing light.

I only have one snowdrop flowering in the garden, the other bulbs are peeping through the ground waiting for their turn. I love it when they eventually all flower and I love to give them away as posies to others and very often the snowdrops will have a personal meaning.

Turn to the snowdrop spirit today and let it bring you new beginnings and hope, strength and healing.

A Message From Gaia

As you approach the winter solstice the gates of the heart are flung open wide and the energies from this very special time will flow into the coming year for this is the time for the greater opening of the heart.
Your hearts are open and you feel so much and you have healed so very much as you have delved deep within to find the fragments from the past which still share their echoes in the present. You have cleared and cleared and cleared again wondering when it would ever stop but the time comes now to move forward and to leave the past behind and to let your heart be your guide as the year turns yet again.
There is only the heart, there has only ever been the heart and there will only ever be the heart and even though your heart may at times feel heavy from all that you endure and from all that you witness in the world outside, your heart will always remain the centre of your being.
When the heart begins to open wider it is then that you move away from the small you into the greater you, further into your own soul light and when this

happens you move further into unity so that your heart light touches the heart light of others.

Some of you may feel vulnerable in opening up yourself in ways that you have not done before and there have been times where you have closed your heart to protect yourself and it was only out of fear and it was meant to be that way but now it is safe to open wide. When you work from the heart your heartbeat beats in tune with mine and it is then that you come into harmony and when there is harmony within there will be harmony without.

You might wonder whether harmony will ever be when you look at the world but I assure you that it is coming. I rise up now more than ever before but as my vibrations quicker then so do the vibrations of everything else and there will be those who will not be able to accept this quickening for it is too painful to be so wide open but there will be others who will open and open and open. When one heart opens it is the same as when a butterfly flaps its wings and the whole universe moves also and when your heart opens so wide the wings of your heart send out vibrations into the world and change happens.

The greatest change comes from the individual who opens to the truth and to the love which comes from the soul and the divine within and when more and more open the love and the light cannot be contained it has to spread.

I open my heart to you all for you were born from me and I am your mother and I hold you in my motherly love and I hold your heart against my heart so that our heartbeats become as one. Feel my love for you my children and take a step further for this winter solstice is all about the further opening of the heart and that is your next step and it is this opening of the greater part of you which sets the scene for the coming year for it is the year of the heart and our two hearts will remain intertwined as we move forward to create a new world.

Yule

I sat the other day and I looked around me in the garden and I saw that there were some stocks, marigolds and snapdragons in flower and although we have climate change now which has altered our seasons I was still in awe at what I was looking at. There was even a foxglove still in flower.
During my walks I have been observing the fattening of the buds on the trees and new leaves coming out on the honeysuckle and all around were signs of spring and yet here we are at the darkest time of the year leading up to the winter solstice.
Even the blue tits have been inspecting the bird boxes and the birds seem to be more active at this time. What a wonderful teaching this for it lets us know that even in the darkest of times there can still be a flowering, there is always hope. The seasons reflect so much back to us and through observing nature we can learn that though the days may be dark there is much new life all around.
The snowdrops are coming through and they are one of the greatest symbols for they not only grow and blossom they also flourish beneath the winter snows

and they are the epitome of hope. There is always hope for us and no matter how you are feeling nature teaches us to remember this and particularly at this time of the year it is her greatest message.

Next week brings the winter solstice with the return of the sun and the birth of the child of the god and the goddess and each day from that date there will be more light in our world. With these last of the darkest days during the coming week look for signs of spring not only around you but within you also, look for the buds of new ways of thinking and new ways of being and keep hold of them and watch them grow and flourish.

I have been cutting back in the garden this week and it reminds me also that there are times where we need to cut back with whatever we are doing and prune some things away and this makes us stronger just like the plants. If you look at a rose tree when it is pruned it is just a few sticks on the ground but yet it holds the potential within it in June to burst into so much beauty. Use this week before the solstice comes to prune and cut back and yet at the same time read the signs and let nature speak to you of her great wisdom and if you cannot get out into nature then go within for she resides within your heart as well and you can journey amongst the budding trees and the bulbs pushing their way out of the earth.

The earth may seem quiet at this moment and yet there is much going on underneath the surface and it is at those times in our own lives when we retreat where there is also much taking place within.

If ever we were to need a symbol of hope to help us in our lives then it would be the earth which would bring us the greatest hope of all. Our great mother is forever and eternally the spirit of hope.

Letting Go

We have had some powerful astrology this weekend and it has set the scene for letting go.
If you could sum up one thing which would epitomise the deep healing many are going through it is letting go and that letting go is one of the hardest things to do. For everything we have experienced in life and all the things which have caused us pain there comes a time to let go but that letting go can only take place when it is time for to let go too soon may mean that you have to revisit again the old things you thought you had dealt with.
We let go every day of our lives, we let go of thoughts, sometimes we let go of people and situations but it is the small things which also are all part of this process. Letting go of clothes and emptying of cupboards, letting go of thoughts of who you think you should be, letting go of thoughts of unworthiness, it is all letting go.
Ram Dass would often say, hold on tightly let go lightly.
What amazing words these are for we hold on so tight to old ways of being and old hurts and so when

freedom calls don't look back look forward then the past has no hold over you any more.

There are many ways you can journey within to practice letting go. You could visualise yourself jumping off a high mountain and feel the fear of it and you will find yourself flying. The old shamans would often use this practice with their students, they would put them into an altered state sometimes using herbs and then they would instruct the student to jump off a cliff.

This never took place in a physical sense but the experience was so strong that the person experiencing it thought it was real.

Every day we can let go a little bit more; don't hold on to possessions which are no longer relevant or which you do not use and do not hold onto thoughts which belong in the past. Do this gently without any guilt and you will put yourself in the flow.

I remember a time in the past when I had a lot of pain in my fingers and it was showing me where I needed to look. I was holding on so tight to old ways of being I wouldn't let go and when I started to let go the pain went also.

So remember hold on tightly let go lightly, renew yourself each day by moving from the past into the new and the greatest newness is always in the mind with the thoughts which we have. Our thoughts are the most powerful things we have so find your freedom by constantly moving forward and change your thoughts as often as you can.

If they is something which is bothering you and you find it hard to let go and if you are ready for it to go see yourself holding on to coloured ribbons which are symbolic of these things and which seem to go out into infinity, hold them tightly and then let go lightly.

The Healing Retreat

I shared this healing journey recently with some of the people I teach and I would like to share it with you also to bring you healing too.

I bring to you the most beautiful healing retreat, a sacred space for you just to be to find healing for what ever you need.

See yourself standing before some gates for they are the entrance to this healing retreat and as you pass through them you leave the world behind. This is such a magical place and it is as vast as your imagination can make it, let your mind expand to create such abundant sacred healing space.

There is a temple surrounded by beautiful gardens and there are healing pools filled with rose petals and many other flowers and herbs for you to bathe in. Go into the healing pools so that you can release any old energies and be renewed with the water element.

There is a little white sanctuary in a quiet corner of the garden, a beautiful circular structure with large arched windows. Inside at the back there is an altar filled with flowers and lit candles and there are soft cushions for you to sit upon as you come here for sanctuary.

Within the temple there are various parts dedicated to different ways of healing and you will also meet many helpers in here waiting for you. They will bring you potions and teas and sacred oils and they will fill you with light and sound as you receive their healing vibrations.

There are soft beds to lie upon where the healing energies are channelled and sacred chants are sung to realign your energies.

There is so much in here to explore so much help for you and each time you enter within there will be new things for you to experience.

You give so much to others it is important also that you give to yourself and that you also take time just for you, just to be to receive. Visit this beautiful place often, sit in the gardens in the sunlight amongst the flowers and the roses and the bathing pools, contemplate in the sanctuary and receive all the healing you need in the temple.

You will never be alone within this beautiful space for there will always be someone waiting for you and not only will they bring you healing they will also be your counsellor so that you can sit with them and pour out your troubles over a healing tea and you will receive all the guidance that you need.

Enjoy your time here and give to yourself for giving to yourself is loving yourself and that will heal you more than anything else.

The Rainbow Fairy

The Earth is fully conscious and is constantly bringing us healing energies and information and at this time she is rising more than ever, her vibrations are quickening and because of this we are more open to communicating with her.

The Earth is both my church and my teacher and she brings me many teachings and she will bring you teachings too if you listen when she calls you.

Yesterday I was very drawn to the deepest green vegetation at the back of a border near my fairyland which I have at the bottom of the garden and I saw emerging from there a round ball of vibrating rainbow light. A sphere of light emerged from the greenery and transformed into a fairy.

We must remember that both the earth and spirit can only communicate with us through our own knowledge and understanding and we see the fairies and angels as beings with wings but this is not the case for they are just vibrations of light and colour.

However we transfer what we have been conditioned to see on to these energies and that is absolutely fine. The form doesn't matter all that matters is the message.

This beautiful fairy being of rainbow light stood in front of me and from her emerged many other fairies and one of them was clothed in orange and I was being brought the orange colour for its teachings and its healing. Along with this I received a beautiful message of how the colours we work with come from the Earth and we connect to them through the plants and flowers and vegetables and all manner of growing things.

I have seen in the past spirals of energy emerge out of the earth for the planet is continuously sending out its light and we can connect to the light to bring us healing as well as to receive messages of wisdom and direction.

The fairy energy is still with me and the rainbow light which it brings. I have always worked with colour and it forms a very strong foundation of all my teachings but now it takes on an even deeper meaning. I share this fairy elemental rainbow light with you and whenever this energy comes to us it brings a lighter energy for it encompasses the element of air which always lifts us up. Each realm and each element brings something different.

Whenever anything with symbolic wings comes to you it is to lift you up.

Go and lie down in your inner journeying upon the green moss in the enchanted forest and receive a healing from the fairies or from the rainbow spheres of light. Go and stand beneath the rainbow waterfall and be cleansed and purified. Sit with the fairies and let them fill you with a lightness of being and let them fill you with the colours of the rainbow and you will be truly blessed.

The Earth is reaching out to us now more than ever and she is sending out healing vibrations and messages and they are there all ready waiting just for you so when you hear your name being called or when you are drawn to investigate an area in your garden or out on your walks then go and look and there you will find magic beyond your wildest dreams.

Miracles

A few days ago a violet flower came into my awareness. I love violets and our garden is full of them; they all came from one plant which a dear friend had given to me.

The violet colour is very special for it is the colour of transformation and magic and many of you will already be familiar with the Violet Flame. It is said that no negativity can exist within the violet colour and the Violet Flame is the flame of transforming old energies into new.

As I connected to the violet which I was shown spiritually I was reminded of something which happened to me a very long time ago. I was going through a very challenging time emotionally and I remembered spending a weekend up in the hills in Northumberland. At the edge of the little town was a gate onto a hillside and that hillside was absolutely covered in violets, it was the most amazing sight and it filled me with wonder.

The night I returned home from my time away something miraculous happened and I was set free from the deep fear which I had been experiencing. I often think of that violet coloured hillside and each time I do it fills me with so much wonder and I associate it with the transformation also of myself at that time.

The violet I was shown the other day revealed this vision to me and I would like to share it with you for your own healing.

Sit quietly and go deep within and you will see a violet coloured door before you and you are to walk through it. As you cross the threshold you will see before you the most glorious countryside and everywhere you look there are carpets of violets.

You walk through the violets and as you move the colours from the violets begin to clothe you so that you find that you are wearing clothes of that colour and it feels absolutely amazing. You can feel all your old energies transformed, they are completely transmuted and you feel an instant change in your energy and it is uplifting and expansive and incredibly healing.

As you look around you see that the violets have all turned to white violets for you have absorbed their colour, this was a gift from the flowers to you.

Mother Earth provides all her colours for us and they all bring their healing qualities and every time you walk past a coloured flower or a green leaved tree you

take that colour in deep within and it brings you
healing without you even realising it.
Bring in the violet flower and the colour when ever
you need the magic of transformation and it will save
you time and time again.

Goddess And God Within

Two people have asked me this week about how they can make a deeper connection to their god goddess self and so I will share this with you as well as you may be looking to deepen your connection too.

Connecting to the goddess god within is about being totally grounded and fully present here on the earth and connecting to your deepest authentic self. It is not about spending hours of meditation or doing courses or immersing yourself in the light it is about contacting and merging with who you truly are.

You do not need to spend long hours of meditation, that belongs in the old ways but yes certainly contemplate and pray to enter into that sacred space but the days are gone when you need to spend hours and days in meditation.

We are moving into a time this year of a much deeper connection to mother Earth for she is rising and reaching out to us to communicate with us to share her teachings and her healing and at the same time we are to be in harmony with her and feel ourselves with our feet upon the ground deeply rooted in this existence. Finding the goddess within is really very ordinary it doesn't require journeys of ascension or looking for a teacher to guide you to yourself all it requires is the full acceptance of who you are with all the masks stripped away.

All those things within you where you have not felt good enough or not as good as another person or not spiritually evolved when you let them go and just see yourself for who you really are then you find your unique magnificent inner self and you realise that all the time you carried god goddess within and all that was required was a recognition of this.

You are magnificent beyond your wildest dreams but that magnificence has been cloaked in so many ways and cloaked through your fear but the cloak can be removed to reveal your ordinary beautiful self. This is what the sacred marriage is all about, this is the union of heaven and earth within, this is your true nature, there was never anything to strive towards there was always just the realisation that you already were that. It is very simple really, it is not complicated and the beauty of the simplicity of it is something which often eludes us and we can have this idea that to claim the goddess within or the god within is something so deeply mystical but it is just very ordinary.

Do not compare yourself to anyone else and do not put any teachers on a pedestal and just know that everyone is striving the same way as you and everyone is searching for home in their own way but we must do this in our own way for someone else's way is not your way.

Sit quietly and strip away all those beliefs about yourself not being good enough, or not good enough spiritually, or you have not been loving enough and tell yourself that you are good enough and you will find your inner beauty and you will love her or him and you will claim your own true self.

All it requires is a recognition and acceptance and then you can stand in your true magnificence and in all your beauty and you can say, I am.

Holidays

During the week I received a Christmas card which had been posted to us from a friend on December 18th, several months previously and the card had been to Bermuda and back, we live in Bermuda Road but it had actually gone to Bermuda.

When I pondered this I was reminded of many years ago when I had a really bad dose of flu and the same friend who had sent the card said that she could see a caravan with me and that I had gone on holiday to be with my higher self. So what I deducted was that I had been spending more time with my higher self during the travels of the card.

We are multi dimensional and there is only part of us here but there are times where we do spend more time with the higher self and if you watch the symbols you will know when those times take place. There are all sorts of reasons for this, maybe you need a rest or a retreat or maybe you need to spend more time learning from the greater part of you.

The colour which connects to the higher self is navy blue and you may have noticed that when you wear that colour you feel more yourself with a deeper connection to who you are. The higher self is your guardian angel for it looks after you continuously and it is the higher self which nudges you to do certain things and to go to certain places and they always make sure that you are in the right place at the right time.

Your higher self is also connected to all the other higher selves of everyone else for it is a field of consciousness this is why we are so deeply connected to one another. This is why synchronicities happen so that people will be drawn to go to the same place at the same time to meet for there will be a purpose to their meeting.

Your higher self will always take care of you and you can talk to it like your best friend and share what you are feeling and you can listen and feel for the response from this other part of you. You can channel messages from your higher self and in fact the further along the path you go the more the information you bring forward comes from there.

This is also the reason why you have access to the energies of the beings you might channel for they are all connected to you. It takes a long time to be connected to your higher self it is not something that happens instantly, it takes a lot of hard work and much time going deep within to get to know yourself and to clear away the old.

You can give your higher self a name if you wish and you can visualise them in any way and you can see them as either male or female and this makes them more accessible to you.

In time it becomes second nature to speak from your higher self to receive from it for a blending takes place gradually until you are fully aligned with it.

So go within and go and meet this greater part of you, spend time getting to know them and receive guidance and information or just go and sit and feel held and loved for they love you more than you could ever begin to imagine. Just think of your guardian angel and that is what your higher self is to you.

The Inner Light

A few days ago as I stepped out of the gate in the back garden I was confronted by a fox and we stood staring at one another for a long time and it was such a beautiful experience. This often happens and I appreciate deeply this wonderful connection.

As I was standing there communicating with the fox there was such a feeling of how the animals see our light, they are drawn to it and it is light which always draws people to us. The animals and the birds feel that light and they are not afraid of us because of this but it is the same with people, people are drawn to us by the light we radiate.

I'm sure that many of you can relate to this and of how time and time again strangers will come and sit by you and talk to you it is if they are drawn like a magnet and indeed they are, they are drawn by the magnetic light which shines from you.

Those that come and speak to us because of what they feel and sense will often receive some comfort and many times they will share their life story even though they are strangers and a kind word to them can make such a difference. However it is not just the kindly words they receive for they also receive light for the light within never empties out, it is the overflowing cup which is always full and we share that light with whoever we come into contact with.

If you look back and see how the birds, bees and butterflies, the animals and people always sought you out you will understand how many times this has happened to you. The light does not belong to us it flows through us wherever we go sharing it for others to receive as well.

I remember a long time ago it was pointed out to me that I hadn't been using my light enough and that I was leaving trails of what symbolically looked like grey dust for when we do not use our light it accumulates around us and it can become heavy and it can make you tired. I soon remedied this by using my light as much as I could and it soon began to flow again.

You do not realise how much light you carry within you, you can't even begin to imagine the magnitude of it, it is truly magnificent. When you are in the company of someone who carries a lot of love and wisdom within them and they don't have to be particularly spiritual, when you are in their field you come away feeling peaceful.

How many times have you shared with another person and felt so much better afterwards and we understand that it is the very act of sharing those things which trouble us which helps to release the old energies we carry within but it is more than this it is the love light from the person you share with that you take away with you.

If only we could see the truth of each other we would see that we are radiant beacons of light and we share that light in the love of humanity.

Past Lives

I include some past life regression in my teaching work but generally I encourage people to work with the issues from their current lives for that is where the healing is. However there are times when you are ready for a past life to be revealed to you and it only ever comes on time and it doesn't come about through looking for it, it comes when the time is right.

With the help of a friend I trust in recent years she has given me insight into lives I have lived which to be honest were horrendous and I now fully understand that my fears and phobias in this life were first conceived in past lives.

This week she felt something with me and she told me that this life she was feeling was the one where all my fears were first conceived and it was at the back of all the lives that I have lived. When I came home after spending time with her I sat down and I told spirit that I was ready to see what ever was waiting to be shown to me and I immediately saw two black lacquered doors and when I stepped through them I found myself out in the universe. In that energy memories from this present life began to be revealed to me, these were all pointers showing me the way to the life I needed to see.

I couldn't sleep that night and again memories from this life kept pouring in, all of them clues to where I had lived and what had happened in the past. I was amazed that I hadn't put all this together before but it hadn't been time.

There are certain things you have been drawn to in your current life and they have without a doubt come from another life and maybe in another culture.

I went back into that life and I discovered when it was and it was a very long time ago. As it was in another culture I googled the history of that culture at that time and what I read blew my mind away for there were so many clues there which related to my phobias in this current life. It absolutely completely astounded me. Very often when we go into a past life where something bad happened to us we do not get involved in the emotion of it we are observers and this is what happened but I also saw a person who had been very prominent in my current life was the one who participated in what had happened to me. I will not go into any details of what took place but it was very frightening.

A couple of days after this Graham suggested we went to the beach to have our lunch from the hut which sells chips there and when we had finished I decided to go for a walk and Graham returned home. It was interesting because before I went out I was drawn to wear a scarf which had feathers on it and when I opened the car door when we arrived there there was an emerald green feather on the floor and I knew without a doubt that I had with me the help of my own soul and helpers.

The heavens opened and it poured with rain and hail stones and the sky was dark and it was the most incredible storm. The tide was in and I stood at the edge of the embankment and all sorts of things poured through me. I often speak to myself when I am out and there was no-one around because the weather was so bad so I let rip.

I actually felt like one of the witches in Macbeth that is what the energy felt like it was so powerful. I emptied out about all that has been done to me in this life and other lives I had lived as well as the one I was immersed in at this time but I also spoke of all those things which had been done to everyone on the planet from other people. I felt completely the injustice of it all.

Upon the spiritual path we have to bring everything back to ourselves and understand what we create for ourselves and the teachings that life provides for us so eventually we do not blame anyone else ever.

However to get to that point we have to allow our own personal feelings for it is by repressing them where we do the damage.

When I had finished I looked at the horizon of the Irish Sea and there was just a small part of a rainbow shining so brightly and from that rainbow there emerged the person whom I have known in this life and who was part of what happened to me in that past life, it was his soul and he took up the whole of the sky. He came to me in ceremonial dress and in his hands he carried a sword and he placed that sword in my hands and I understood completely what it meant. It was the returning to me of a part of myself with all it symbolised for we leave parts of ourselves in other lives and when the time is right we reclaim those parts back.

What has amazed me as well as all this is that aspects of that culture which I lived in then have come to the surface in the last couple of weeks, they seem to be coming in to my healing work and this is what happens when we connect to a past life for we not only gain the understanding of what makes us as we are we also open the door to our own teachings which we have gathered in that life.

When I had completed everything I walked back home absolutely soaked through from the storm but by the time I arrived home the sun had come out. I share this with you to help you to understand that when it is time the reasons behind things you have had to deal with in this life time will be shown to you and only when it is time. Also those deepest emotions within you which may cause you such fear and terror although they come from all you have dealt with in this current life they have their roots in the past.

I said to my friend that all the fear I have suffered in this life has made me more compassionate towards others and she turned to me and she said that I had not come here to learn compassion for others I had come to learn compassion for myself.

Her words rang so true for I feel more compassion for myself now for what I have discovered so be compassionate to yourself as well for those things which you find hard to overcome. Love yourself and nurture yourself and have compassion and respect for yourself because no matter what you have endured your heart is still open and you help so many others just by being you.

The Garden Of The Soul

Last year on two occasions within a week when I was buying plants at two different garden centres people came up to me thinking that I worked there. As I contemplated what that meant and the symbolism of this I deducted that it was just showing me that the spiritual work that I do is like a garden. I had already realised this many years ago but it brought it home again.

The memory of this has come back to me again recently and it reminded me that my grandfather was a head gardener on a country estate at a place called Eden Hill near Cork and he ran off with the daughter of the big house. So my father was brought up with country ways and he had many stories to tell us.

My teachings have always been very much based upon nature and as I always say and I know that many of you say this as well that nature is my church and the teachings from my soul are in fact teachings from an enormous garden. We can see the soul in many ways and it all depends on our personal preferences. You may like to see your soul as a temple or even a church but for me it is a garden.

In the garden of my soul it is filled with the beauty of all the flowers there and I have had a passion for flowers for the whole of my life. There is so much in here, there is water, there are trees, there are many plants and herbs but it is also a place where I actually meet my own higher self within my soul energy. I can also meet my guides and remember that some of our guides are our selves from other lives.

The soul is vast beyond anything we could ever even begin to imagine, there is no way our limited human mind could even begin to understand the unlimited energy of it but we can still enter into our souls and you will know when you do this for the energy is so peaceful. For a long time there have been times where I have sat quietly and a great stillness has descended around me and I always know that I have entered into my soul light when this happens.

Go into your own soul and see it as a garden or temple or a vast landscape and you may even like to go through a door to enter within so that you feel that you are really crossing through the veil. Go into that space and explore it there and you will find healing, teachings and comfort or whatever it is that you need at any time.

We are working in the new energy now and it is so different for we are very much working in the soul state and with the souls of others and in truth there is no separation between us anyway.

I have always loved to see the analogy of the garden as symbolic of the healing work we do for we weed out the old thoughts, we compost them and transform them and we plant new seeds and we nurture them with the elements as they grow and blossom and fruit. We are the gardeners of our own lives and the lives of those whom we help.

Go into your soul today for it is only a thought away.

The Healer Within

More and more in our spiritual work in all our
teachings healing will become more important than
ever. We heal others in so many ways, we heal with
the wisdom we share with others and we heal by
sharing all the different methods of creating balance
within the body. We heal when we put our hands on
another person and channel the light and we can also
heal ourselves in the same way.

Any emotions which you have not been able to process
lodge within the energy body and ultimately in the
physical body and there they will manifest a symptom
or pain or discomfort letting you know where to look
to bring balance back. We are made of energy and just
as our thoughts can create energy blockages then our
intentions can also release those blockages and create a
greater flow of light within.

We can heal ourselves first and foremost by going to
the roots of all those things we have been dealing with
and heal the emotions which were first created at the
very beginning when they were conceived. When we
discover them and feel them completely we can then

release and transform the energies which have been held within the physical body for a very long time.

We can also heal ourselves by working with our own energies for very often within the body the energy flows will become out of balance with either too much energy flowing or too little or where the energy dams up like a river. We can create a greater flow within by moving those energies so that everything flows to bring the light to every part of our being.

Everyone has the ability to heal not only others but also themselves and you can place your hands upon any pain or discomfort you have and channel the light. It is often good to rub your hands together before you begin and then place them over any part of you which you feel needs healing. Once you begin to do this your intuition begins to expand and your hands may be drawn to another part of your body to channel healing there also. The more you do this the more you become aware of the energies within your body and we can work with those energies by drawing out anything which is stagnant, holding it in our hands, looking into it and feeling what emotions have been held in and then we can transform that energy and put it back into the body as healing light.

What you must never do is to take energy from yourself or anyone else you are healing and discard it for you will leave it lying around for someone else to pick up or you may even magnetise it back to yourself so you always transform what ever you release and you put it back as light.

Work on your physical body if you have pain and discomfort and if you have emotional pain then work upon your heart centre. If your mind feels confused or foggy then work within the aura of the head. Use your hands to feel the energy and work with it to move the energy. You can also do the same within your chakras drawing out the old energy with your hands and then feeling it, transforming it and putting it back as radiant light.

You can work with your aura by running your hands through it to make sure it is vibrant and expansive because sometimes we draw our auras further in if life is too challenging. Expand your aura and use your hands to do this drawing the energy out and then you can smooth your aura down with your hands for it can also become ruffled due to what ever we are dealing with.

Become your own healer and use your daily practices to heal yourself and you will be amazed at the results and when you begin to move the energies within your energy body you may find that old thoughts come to the surface for you have released them from their holding stations within your energy field. So feel and heal.

Working with your energies in this way will have an effect upon your physical body and you will notice a difference immediately for you can change energy instantly. This is the time for healing and it will continue to be a greater part of all the work that we do as we move into the future. As we are not separate from anything the more healing we do on ourselves the more healing that the Earth receives also for there is always an exchange of energy between us and Gaia.

Destiny

I began my spiritual journey many years ago and I have just found out that my first teacher has passed away and it brought back to me memories from the very beginning of my journey. I am so grateful to everyone who has helped me along this path and I'm grateful to the teachers whom I have met along the way. My first teacher introduced me to Indian spirituality and it is always said that you always return to your first love and my first love was Hinduism.
A group of us would meditate together every week and sometimes for days at weekends and many friendships were forged through coming together with common interests. Much water has passed under the bridge since then and I met another teacher who helped me to develop as a medium and to also help me in my own personal healing.
There are many who walk with us upon the spiritual path, some come just for a short time and others are always there but each person has a purpose whether those connections are painful or harmonious it is all about what we learn from every experience.

Long gone are the days where I would sit for hours in meditation for that is not needed now, we are working in a new energy for the new earth. I have no regrets about all the things I experienced and I am forever grateful for the wonderful foundation of spiritual teachings which I received from my first teacher.

We are our own teachers now and even though we need to reach out for help at times and we all need support at certain moments but it is more to the inner teacher within where we go whether that is your own higher self or your guides who are part of you. Mary Magdalene's greatest message was that everything you need to know is within and that is as true now as it was 2000 years ago.

It is good to reflect back upon your journey and to remember all the things which have brought you to this point and of how synchronicity is always at work. I owned a health food shop when I first met the person I'm speaking about and the minute he walked into it I knew him and so it was destined that our paths would cross for a certain time. These things are always destined; the meetings which seem to happen by chance are all designed for our awakening.

There is so much beauty in life and the way that everything comes together that we meet certain people at the right time for whatever we need to learn. We are all linked as one and our higher selves are all part of the oneness this is why there are divine appointments at certain times in your life where you meet people who will change the course of your life.

From the moment I first began my spiritual journey in earnest I was smitten and I could never get enough of the knowledge which others shared with me and from the books which I read.

So much has changed upon the spiritual path for we have now come to a point where we are bringing heaven to earth so that there is no separation and we live our lives totally immersed in the light of the divine everyday and we are also all part of the divine light. We don't need to sit in a cave or sit for hours meditating all we need to do is to open our hearts to one another and the divinity within each person. Namaste.

Spring

Today is the day of the Spring Equinox where day and night are of equal length and it is a day of balance as well as new beginnings and rebirth. We were born from mother Earth and we are part of her and when we are in harmony with her rhythms we create inner harmony too. The ancients knew the secrets of living according to the seasons and the cycles of each year and their lives reflected the continuous change which they observed in the landscape.

We create balance by living in harmony with one another but there is another type of balance and that is when we live in harmony with both heaven and earth. Ascension and the new earth are not about going anywhere or lifting up to somewhere higher it is about bringing heaven to earth which is symbolic of higher consciousness. We bring in the light and we carry that light within us and that light spreads into the Earth as well as amongst those whom we come into contact with.

The number eight which is also a symbol of infinity and a symbol of the high priestess and the magician carries within it the bringing of heaven to earth. In the

Far East it is considered a very fortunate number as it is all about balance.

The more grounded we become here the more we bring in the higher energies and we see divinity in everything around us. The Earth heals us not only with her healing herbs but with the colours which she provides through all her flowers and just to be amongst flowers brings you healing. The colours from the flowers bring a rainbow of light to the body and mind creating healing for what ever you need.

When I go into the garden or out into the wildness of nature I am in paradise, this is my heaven on earth and I recognise the healing energies which the great goddess provides for us.

Sometimes I say to people, come and sit with me in the garden in the soul state and sometimes I will see someone who just appears without any prompting from me and I see them sitting in the chair next to me in the quietness to receive the healing. We can certainly be in more than one place at once.

On this beautiful day of the balance of light and dark on the day of new beginnings if you need healing, come and sit with me next to the flowers and take in their colours and you will have the rainbow within and that rainbow will go to where ever you need healing and the essence of the flowers will bring you healing too. There is much magic in nature, much healing to be received and all we need to do is to connect and to recognise that we are in the presence of heaven brought to earth.

So if you need healing, sit by me in the garden and take in the colours of the flowers and we will listen to the sound of the water in the water feature, we will hear the birds sing and we will watch them as they eat from the birdfeeder and set up home in the nest boxes, we will drink tea and eat cake and enjoy the peace and harmony and the healing of our great mother.

The Greening

Some time ago Merlin brought me emerald fire from deep within the earth and this emerald fire carried the deepest healing. I knew that this fire was very important for the new earth and that the colour of it was very significant for even though we understand what the green means it has a much deeper meaning than we yet know about.

St. Hidegard of Bingen a 12th century saint who had incredible knowledge of the healing powers of the natural world used the phrase viriditas and she referred to this as the greening. It was the greening power of nature but this meaning went far beyond that, it was the divinity which is within all things and which is within the greening. It is the life force within plants but it is also the light and the life which we receive from spirit.

We understand that when we go out into nature or into the forests or the woods the green brings healing and balance and harmony but it is much more than this for you are actually connecting to the rising of the divinity which is within all things.

I have spoken about the emerald fire before and I know that it is very much part of our journey into the new earth, a journey which has already begun and will continue. When Merlin brought the emerald fire to me from deep within the earth the symbolism of this was that something so powerful was being shared with us which came from the depths of consciousness, it was something which was being brought into the light of day. This emerald fire can bring you much healing and all you need

to do is to stand within it and fill up with it and let it flow
through every part of you.

You can receive the same vibration of it if you make a
connection to the plants and you can do this either by being
amongst plants or by using them to make teas and tinctures or
many other things. You are receiving the greening every time
you take in a herbal remedy.

This time of year, the springtime, is when the life force rises
everywhere in nature and there is much potent medicine to be
received by being in tune with everything which is around you.
We can look at the colour green and know that it is a healing
colour, it is the colour of harmony and it is also a colour which
connects us to the etheric realms and to the ancient mysteries
but now it is important that we look at it as the greening power
of the divine.

Divinity is everywhere and nature has consciousness this is why
we can communicate with any of the realms of the Earth and
receive healing messages and as we move forwards to create
heaven on earth there will be no separation between us and the
plants. Shamans have known this since very ancient times but it
will become natural to everyone when we understand that we
are not separate from anything or anyone.

Step into the greening the creative power of life and you will be
filled with abundant healing and a greater knowledge of the
medicine of the divine.

About The Author

Margaret Hunt has been a spiritual teacher, a medium and a healer for many years.

Her first career was as a schoolteacher and she followed this as the owner of a health food shop where she was able to follow her passion of healing and spiritual awakening.

She is qualified not only as a teacher but also as a Dietary Therapist and a Touch For Health Therapist; Margaret also practised Black Hat Feng Shui and she spent 10 years as a volunteer dietician with Wirral Holistic Care Services.

She set up a school to train Magdalene Priestesses and Magdalene High Priestesses and she ran many Magdalene Retreat Days in the UK alongside training people to be Flower Power Healing Practitioners and also providing Goddess Mentoring, a year long programme.

Margaret specialises in healing the emotional body and as well as teaching and running courses she also works with clients on a one-to-one basis.

Margaret's passion is to help people to become their own healers by releasing and understanding all the emotions they have experienced throughout their lifetime enabling them to be reborn again in self-love and self empowerment.

She has a passion for the natural world loving nothing better than to be out in her garden tending her roses and cottage garden flowers and herbs or to be out in the woods and the lanes communing with mother earth.

As a daughter of an Irish countryman she was brought up on tales of the elementals and of the bounty of nature's rich remedies and her mother was as passionate about nature as her father and she loved roses too.

She communicates directly with the plant world bringing messages from everything around her and translating the spiritual symbolism of all things, the language of light, to whoever needs it.

Margaret knows without a doubt that we are now working in a new energy creating a New Earth where peace and harmony will eventually come and she brings together those working in the light with love for humanity and the new world to come.

www.newearthsisterhood.co.uk
mm@newearthsisterhood.co.uk

Printed in Great Britain
by Amazon

13500522R00210